DIGITAL GAMES

AATE Interface Series
Series Editor: Cal Durrant

The AATE/Interface series comprises a range of books for teachers who are committed to researching their own teaching – teachers who work at the interface between theory and practice. Interface titles all have a practical edge, in that they include ideas developed in the classrooms, for use in the classrooms. Yet they are far more than a set of resources. The primary purpose of the AATE/Interface series is to address significant issues in English curriculum and pedagogy, and as such it represents a substantial contribution to our knowledge as English teachers and literacy educators. To date, the series consists of:

Teenagers and Reading: Literary Heritages, Cultural Contexts and Contemporary Reading Practices
Edited by Jacqueline Manual and Sue Brindley 2012

Teaching Aus Literature: From Classroom Conversations to National Imaginings
Edited by Brenton Doecke, Larissa McLean Davies and Philip Mead 2011

English for a New Millennium: Leading Change
Edited by Cal Durrant and Karen Starr 2009

Media Teaching: Language, Audience and Production
Edited by Andrew Burn and Cal Durrant 2008

'Only Connect …': English Teaching, Schooling and Community
Edited by Brenton Doecke, Mark Howie and Wayne Sawyer 2006

Writing=Learning
Edited by Brenton Doecke and Graham Parr 2005

English Teachers at Work: Narratives, Counter Narratives and Arguments
Edited by Brenton Doecke, David Homer and Helen Nixon 2003

Empowering Readers: Ten Approaches to Narrative
Garry Gillard, with a foreword by Alec McHoul 2002

For All Time? Critical Issues in Teaching Shakespeare
Edited by Paul Skrebels and Sieta van der Hoeven,
with a foreword by John Bell 2002

P(ICT)ures of English: Teachers, Learners and Technology
Edited by Cal Durrant and Catherine Beavis 2001

Relocating the Personal: A Critical Writing Pedagogy
Barbara Kamler with a foreword by Michelle Fine 2001

Exploring Narrative: A Guide to Teaching 'The Girl who Married a Fly' and Other Stories
Val Kent with a contribution by Ray Misson 2000

Responding to Students' Writing: Continuing Conversations
Edited by Brenton Doecke with an introduction by Margaret Gill 1999

Gender and Texts: A Professional Development Package for English Teachers
Edited by Wayne Martino and Chris Cook 1998

DIGITAL GAMES
LITERACY IN ACTION

**CATHERINE BEAVIS, JOANNE O'MARA
AND LISA MCNEICE (EDS)**

Wakefield Press

Wakefield Press
1 The Parade West
Kent Town
South Australia 5067
www.wakefieldpress.com.au

in association with

The Australian Association for the Teaching of English
416 Magill Road
Kensington Gardens
South Australia 5068
www.aate.org.au

First published 2012

Copyright © Australian Association for the Teaching of English, 2012

All rights reserved. This book is copyright. Apart from any fair dealing for the purposes of private study, research, criticism or review, as permitted under the Copyright Act, no part may be reproduced without written permission. Enquiries should be addressed to the publisher.

AATE has endeavoured to seek permission to use any material which may be copyright. In some cases we have not received replies to our requests. We would be grateful for any information that would assist us in this task.

AATE Interface Series Editor: Cal Durrant

Cover designed by Stacey Zass
Designed and typeset by Wakefield Press
Printed and bound by Hyde Park Press, Adelaide

National Library of Australia Cataloguing-in-Publication entry

Title:	Digital games: literacy in action / edited by Catherine Beavis; Joanne O'Mara and Lisa McNeice.
ISBN:	978 1 74305 127 6 (pbk.).
Series:	AATE interface series.
Notes:	Includes index.
Subjects:	Computers and literacy – Australia.
	Education – Effect of technological innovations on.
	Visual literacy.
	Video games and children.
Other Authors/ Contributors:	Beavis, Catherine.
	O'Mara, Joanne.
	McNeice, Lisa.
Dewey Number:	302.22440285

Contents

Acknowledgements		vii
Preface	Play up! play up! and play the game!: Digital games and the literacy boomerang *Cal Durrant*	ix
Foreword	*Louise Dressing, Gael McIndoe and Debbie de Laps*	xvii

Part 1 – Framing chapters

Chapter 1	Literacy learning and computer games: A curriculum challenge for our times *Catherine Beavis, Joanne O'Mara and Lisa McNeice*	3
Chapter 2	A model for games and literacy *Catherine Beavis and Thomas Apperley*	12

Part 2 – Perspectives from the classroom

Chapter 3	Computer games, archetypes and the quest narrative: Computer games as texts in the Year 9 English classroom *Lisa McNeice, Andrea Smith and Toby Robison*	24
Chapter 4	Breaking through the fourth wall: Invitation from an avatar *Joanne O'Mara and Belinda Lees*	33
Chapter 5	'Gamer hands': Console games as texts and activities that use gaming as a stimulus *Mark Cuddon*	41
Chapter 6	Literacy, identity and online fantasy sports games *Amanda Gutierrez and Catherine Beavis*	50
Chapter 7	A blank slate: Using *GameMaker* to create computer games *Joanne O'Mara and John Richards*	57
Chapter 8	Game plan: Using computer games in English class to engage the disengaged *Paul Byrne*	65

| Chapter 9 | Reading in the digital age
Frank Ferretti | 73 |
| Chapter 10 | *Game-O-Rama!*
Maureen Cann | 81 |

Part 3 – Extending work with games

| Chapter 11 | Including serious games in the classroom
Christopher S. Walsh | 94 |

Part 4 – Perspectives from beyond the classroom

Chapter 12	Computer games and the after-school club *Jeanette Hannaford*	108
Chapter 13	Narrative and computer games *Clare Bradford*	115
Chapter 14	Videogames and innovation *Vincent Trundle*	121
Chapter 15	Gender and computer games: What can we learn from the research? *Claire Charles*	127

Part 5 – Resources

References	136
Print and online resources	144
Appendix	148

| Index | 151 |

Acknowledgements

A longer version of Chapter 6, Literacy, Identity and Online Fantasy Games, first appeared as 'Experts on the field': redefining literacy boundaries. In Donna Alvermann, Ed. (2010) *Adololescents' online literacies: Connecting classrooms, digital media and popular culture* (pp. 145-162). Peter Lang, New York.

Photographs: Jacqueline Gith, Julie Langlands
Editorial assistance and Model design: Joy Reynolds

Preface
Play up! play up! and play the game!
Digital games and the literacy boomerang
Cal Durrant

In January of 1995, the Australian Association for the Teaching of English (AATE) national conference was held at North Sydney Boys High School. The weather was warm and sunny, and the mid-north coast beaches beckoned me away from Armidale, but I was keen to hear Myron Tuman, author of *Word perfect: Literacy in the computer age* (1992), as I'd been involved in getting him to the conference, so down to Sydney I dutifully went. During a lull between keynotes, I noticed in the program a presentation by Catherine Beavis and Terry Hayes on something called the *Prince of Persia*. Although I had recently become interested in the ways computer technology was impacting on English classrooms (e.g., Durrant, 1995), I had not thought much to that point about computer games as sources of textual study, so I found the school based research that Catherine was conducting with Terry Hayes' Year 8s at Hawthorn Secondary College quite fascinating.

Those tentative beginnings in the early 1990s have now expanded into the richly theorised model that we see in evidence throughout this book. For someone interested in the uneasy and complex relationships between computers and English teachers over the past three decades (see Durrant, 2001; Durrant & Hargreaves, 1995, 1996), I think it's important to reflect on just where computer games might fit within the literacy spaces that have opened up during that period.

Recently, I came across Miles Myers' discussion paper entitled: *The present literacy crisis and the public interest* (Myers, 1986). During the 1980s, Myers was President of the Californian Federation of Teachers, Chair of the Trustees of the National Council of Teachers of English (NCTE) and Co-Director in charge of Evaluation of the Bay Area Writing Project (Myers, 1987, p. 4). His paper addressed yet another 'literacy crisis' in the United States and took the unusual position that literacy crises evolve from a record of school successes rather than failures because the achievement of each new standard of literacy contributes to the pressure for yet higher standards and an almost inevitable newly perceived crisis in the next cycle (p. 17).

I have described elsewhere (Durrant, 2012) the various literacy stages that Myers suggested have existed in the United States since the beginning of the 19th century, so I will merely sketch them here. He noted that in 1800 the US required its citizens to be fluent speakers (Oral literacy) but that by the middle of the 19th century, they needed to be able to sign their names (Signature literacy) as part of the demands of a new agrarian economy with a population largely transient between eastern and western seaboards, a scenario not so unlike the situation in the Australian colonies at that time, though perhaps for different reasons (Myers, 1986, p. 3).

In addition, there had been a major intake of migrants into the United States by this time and schools were being pressured to add a new form of literacy to previous requirements, that of Recitation literacy as a means of socialising the children of these newcomers into the ways and values of their adopted country. This form of literacy required children to 'recite passages from core texts of the culture' as a means of demonstrating their acknowledgement of what being a US citizen meant (p. 4).

The American involvement in World War I saw new literacy demands move towards basic Sign literacy as part of a shift to what Myers called Comprehension literacy. Without the capacity to make sense of the relationships between letters and sounds, or to read signs and labels, it was difficult for the population to be active members of organised armies, factories or markets. Interestingly enough, critics argued that this new emphasis on print literacy was something that was going to lead over time to 'a general loss of memory and a general decline in intelligence' of the American population (p. 5). Unsurprisingly, this is not an argument restricted to this period of American education; other educational alarmists have marshalled similar arguments against newer thinking about and approaches to literacy (see for example, Donnelly, 2004, 2005 on Critical literacy).

Myers asserts that while Sign literacy was sufficient during and immediately after World War II, by the time of the Vietnam conflict, it was no longer perceived as being enough. A full shift to Comprehension literacy was now required, and the pressure for this came with the launch of Russia's Sputnik in 1957. Myers suggested that this event demonstrated to all Americans that simple skills in phonics and signs would not cut it in the new space age; more advanced literacy skills around the summarising of literal information was now needed. Not only this, but in order to achieve such gains, new models of teaching were required, and so behaviourist forms of learning were introduced to American schools whereby skills and drills became the norm and teachers were encouraged to implement stimulus-response materials prepared and supplied by centralised agencies (p. 7).

But between the 1950s and the 1980s, critics began to suggest that undue emphasis on Comprehension literacy was exposing American students to manipulation by authors of printed texts, and so the idea of developing Inferential literacy was proposed. It is interesting to note that this was not an exclusively educational directive. Rather it was done in recognition that market driven economies required literate workers capable of making informed decisions not just in their personal lives but also in the context of the workplace. Such development would produce a workforce with the capacity to move flexibly between jobs as well as meet changing job demands. It is not unlike the multiple imperatives for Australian students outlined by documents such as the 1989 Hobart Declaration (Ministerial Council for Education, Employment, Training and Youth Affairs (MCEETYA), 1999), where one of the aims for the Common and Agreed National Goals for Schooling in Australia was:

> *To respond to the current and emerging economic and social needs of the nation, and to provide those skills which will allow students maximum flexibility and adaptability in their future employment and other aspects of life.*

Myers' literacy progression is summarised below in Figure 1.

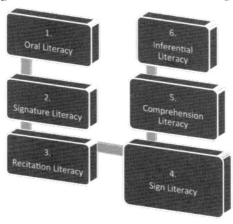

Figure 1. The Miles Myers Literacy Stages *(After Myers, 1986)*

Digital games: Literacy in action

Over a decade ago, Bill Green and I used a similar set of progressions in our discussion around literacy in 3D and the new technologies in education (Durrant and Green, 2000), based on Chip Bruce's description in Figure 2.

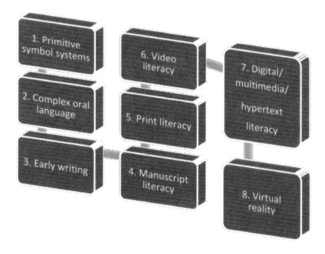

Figure 2. The Chip Bruce Literacy Stages *(After Bruce, 1998)*

In Figure 3, I have conflated these two overviews of literacy developments onto what I have called elsewhere the 'Literacy Boomerang' (Durrant, 2012). Framing the Boomerang are Myers' Literacy development stages that run along the bottom of the diagram from Oral literacy on the left to Comprehension literacy on the right. This is then picked up again across the top of the frame commencing with Comprehension literacy in the top right corner through to the additions I have included encompassing Web 1.0, 2.0 and 3.0 literacies in the top left corner.

Readers are possibly familiar with the terms Web 1.0, 2.0 and 3.0 and the types of literacies associated with them. Web 1.0 principally comprises content material on the internet; it is very much a one-way communication process where the user searches for 'information', which was mostly print based in nature when it began during the early 1990s. Web 2.0 is variously referred to as Social networking or the social Web; *Facebook* and *YouTube* are perhaps the most recognisable services provided, and the literacy demands move away from mere information retrieval to interactional sharing via text, video and screen. Web 3.0 is less easily definable, but appears to be characterised by advances on Web 2.0 services in the sense that everything is designed to be smaller, faster, more flexible across platforms and devices, more mobile

Play up! Play up! and play the game!

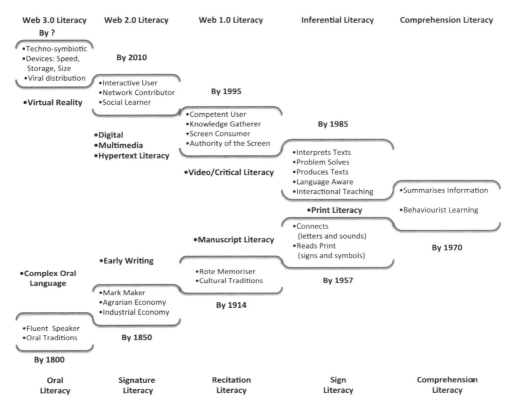

Figure 3. The Literacy Boomerang (Durrant, 2012)
After Bruce (1998) and Myers (1986)

and also virally distributed, i.e. through apps, email, and other yet to be invented social networks (Armstrong, 2009, p. 954). There is also likely to be a more symbiotic relationship between computers and humans as part of this phase, not in a conspiratorial or sinister sense, but after what some have recently referred to as Techno-symbiosis, where technology is recognised as a type of natural extension of humans, a sort of computer/human cohabitation (Brangiere & Hammes-Adele, 2011).

The Literacy Boomerang itself comprises two edges. The inside curve uses Bruce's literacy development stages, and these align with Myers' horizontal frames; the boomerang shape assists in separating Myers' Sign, Comprehension and Inferential literacies but allows all three to be included in Bruce's Print Literacy stage on the inside curve.

The outside edge of the curve simply approximates the years when the accompanying stages are generally acknowledged to have occurred, though of course such approximations vary according to geographical locations. As with any dating principle in relation to literacy practices, at least two things should be kept firmly in mind. First, there is no assertion here that these dates are exact; they are merely approximate indicators. Second, neither is there any suggestion that each new literacy development entirely 'replaces' the previous one; rather, that each new literacy stage subsumes all previous stages. It would be foolish to assert that the practices of one period entirely replace the practices of previous stages – if this was the case, we would be reinventing the wheel over and over. Clearly, they are absorbed by, adapted to or improved by the new technologies and ideas that become available over time. My scribbled notes with a ballpoint are certainly different from, yet entirely historically traceable to – technologically speaking – the blackened stick marks made on cave walls by our ancestors. Despite the demise of the typewriter, its residual impacts are also clearly visible on the latest computer keyboards. What is fascinating about an overview of such developments is that the further we extend along the upper arm of the Literacy Boomerang, the more we seem to be reverting to the agencies and statuses of earlier literacy focal points. For example, as voice recognition software is further refined in both mobile telecommunications as well as desktop, laptop and tablet applications, we likely will see an increase in Oral literacy emphases in schooling practices to enable students to maximise their usage of the long-promised generations of keyboard-less computers.

Returning to Figure 3, the 'flat' surface of the Boomerang indicated within the interlocking curved lines contains abbreviated examples of the identifying characteristics of literacy users of that period accompanied by some of the economic and cultural pressures that helped shape such practices. Once again, few of these periods just 'stopped' when another began; in nearly all cases they have involved fierce struggles for dominance, not just about philosophical and cultural differences, but often in the service of powerful economic forces that have followed every movement with an eye for gaining market advantages over their own rivals. For me, this best explains the succession of literacy crises that we have seen promoted over the past one hundred years: the new hounding out the old, and the old mustering powerful cultural and economic allies to resist their own displacement and subverting the new by waging campaigns about the apparent inadequacies of the new over the old. We have all seen such 'back to basics' or 'golden ages' (that never were) campaigns in operation. They have limited value in terms of resistance to

Play up! Play up! and play the game!

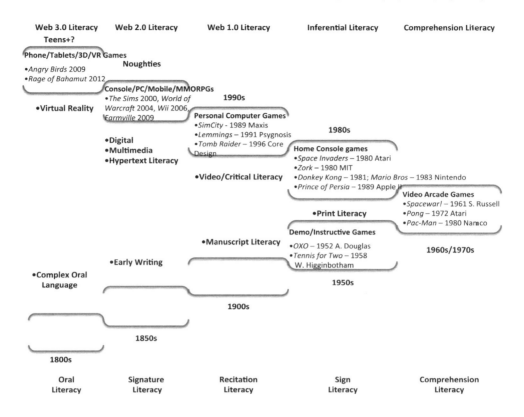

Figure 4. The Literacy Boomerang and Digital Games

change, and I can't think of a really innovative literacy practice or idea that has not won out in the end, and many of these are included in the diagram.

But what of digital gaming and literacy?

In Figure 4, I have replaced the descriptive boxes referred to above with a metaphorical 'adhesive overlay' for the Literacy Boomerang showing the digital games developments since the 1950s. While I am not suggesting that these match the Myers frame particularly closely as far as the types of literacy progressions go, they do approximate the same time periods, showing a rapidly developing complexity both in the game playing 'literacy' required to engage in the action and the increased levels of speed, graphic detail and realism accompanying such gaming. Perhaps it might be best thought of as an 'app' for the Literacy Boomerang! I remember well the introduction of *Pong* into the pinball arcades during the 1970s; it was very impressive and great fun to play, but also a very different experience from engaging in the multiplayer online games so popular now.

As I travel the public transport system around Sydney's inner west, it is a rare sight indeed to see school aged children sitting on a seat taking in the view. Most of them are listening to DAPs (Digital Audio Players) of one form or another, surfing the internet or playing games on tablets or mobile phones – or doing all three. This is the generation that currently inhabits school classrooms. The next generation is characterised by the well known *YouTube* clip, *A Magazine is an iPad that does not work.m4v*, where a baby is shown using an iPad and then becoming frustrated as she fails to get a variety of print magazine pages to 'work' by using the same hand movements (http://www.youtube.com/watch?v=aXV-yaFmQNk). Some teachers see this kind of technological shift as very confronting. Yet I watch my 18 month old grand daughter whose father manages the ICT programs across a primary and secondary school complex servicing approximately a thousand students; she is surrounded by electronic gadgetry of every description, yet despite her interest in these, she remains entranced by traditional book forms.

And perhaps that is what makes this book so timely and relevant. What should English teachers be looking for in terms of theoretical guidance for their teaching; how should they be approaching the use of digital games in their classrooms, and what are the experiences of their peers who have ventured forth and focused on games as text as well as action in subject English? This book goes a long way towards providing definitive answers and direction to such 'big' questions.

As a consequence, AATE is proud to be a partner in assisting this text through the publishing process, and those of us on Council are confident that it will prove to be one of the most popular and well-used texts in our *Interface* Series. Our thanks then to the editorial team, Catherine Beavis, Joanne O'Mara and Lisa McNeice for their foresight and tenacity in seeing this project through, and to the various industry partners who have backed this crucial research. It is yet another example of the significant advantages to be gained from collaborative project work amongst school, academic and industry personnel. I trust that you as reader will gain much from engaging with and digesting the contents of this text and am confident that you will revisit it many times over.

Cal Durrant
AATE Commissioning Editor
Associate Professor and Director: The ACU Literacy Research Hub

Foreword

Louise Dressing, Gael McIndoe and Debbie de Laps

This book has emerged from the Australian Research Council-funded Linkage project, *Literacy in the Digital World of the Twenty-First Century: Learning from Computer Games*. This project was funded under the Linkage Projects scheme. As the Australian Research Council website explains, Linkage Projects:

> *support research and development projects which are collaborative between higher education researchers and other parts of the national innovation system, which are undertaken to acquire new knowledge, and which involve risk or innovation. (Australian Research Council, 2011)*

In this instance, the partnership was between the research team based at Deakin University, the Department of Education and Early Childhood Development in Victoria, The Australian Association for the Moving Image, and the Victorian Association for the Teaching of English.

A fundamental objective of the *Linkage Projects* scheme is to

> *encourage and develop long-term strategic research alliances between higher education organisations and other organisations, including with industry and other end-users, in order to apply advanced knowledge to problems and/or to provide opportunities to obtain national economic, social or cultural benefits. (Australian Research Council, 2011)*

As we outline below, the development of deeper understandings of contemporary digital forms, and of young people's engagement with them, and of the forms that digital literacy takes in new media phenomena such as computer games, is essential if teachers and other professionals are to help prepare young people to be critical and capable analysts, users and creators of 21st century literacies. This priority is central, in different but complementary ways, to each of the Industry Partner Organisations represented here.

Important outcomes of the project were the development of a model for computer games literacies and resources to support curriculum planning and pedagogy in this area. This book presents the model, teacher case studies, and a range of resources and perspectives for teaching with and about computer games. As Industry Partners we are pleased to have the opportunity to introduce it, and hope that readers will find in it a wealth of insights, resources and ideas to support them in their work with young people and contemporary literacies.

Department of Education and Early Childhood Development

While literacy has ever been a traditional focus of educators, computer games and gaming are at the cutting edge of what is considered within the legitimate realm of education. So to have even posed such questions as: *What kinds of literacy and learning practices are adolescents involved in as they play computer games?* and *What do computer games and adolescents' engagement with them have to teach us about how to teach both print and multimodal texts and literacies?* bespeaks both a brave and exciting investigation of which this book of case studies is one of the outcomes.

For young people to be fully literate in the 21st century, they need to become capable and critical users of both print and multimodal literacy, and to bring informed and analytic perspectives to bear on all texts, both print and digital, that they encounter with increasing frequency in everyday life. The challenge for educators has been to build connections between school and the world beyond, to meet the needs of all students and to counter the disengagement common in the middle years. Making the curriculum relevant to the needs and preferences of the learners, and listening to their preferences and the way they use new technologies out of school is the challenge the *Digital Games: Literacy in Action* addresses.

Of particular value is the conceptual way of thinking about gaming; the texts around gaming and the ways gaming fosters attitudes towards learning, organising, knowledge sharing and collaboration, as a way of providing for planning and pedagogy, to be used in professional development programs. The development of the theoretical model: *Games as text, games as action* by Tom Apperley and Catherine Beavis, reflecting the interdisciplinary nature of the field, locates the case studies in a sound theoretical framework through which to conceptualise games and gaming. This will help teachers to develop innovative curriculum and pedagogy in the future that both engages and challenges young people.

The Department of Education and Early Childhood Development in Victoria (DEECD) supports a range of collaborative research projects with practitioners, university and industry partners. This project has been valuable for DEECD because it is innovative and future focused, seeking to explore how students and teachers can make the most of emerging technologies. The products – new knowledge and resources for teaching and professional development – will be of considerable value to teachers and curriculum leaders.

Australian Centre for the Moving Image

One of the key challenges facing the educators in the digital age is ensuring we create the capacity to initiate what Kevin Kelly has described as a shift from 'book fluency to screen fluency, from literacy to visuality' (Kelly, 2008). Pivotal to this shift is the need for educational paradigms to transcend the comfortable and familiar notations of literacy (both print and screen) and move towards a 'transliteracy,' empowering the evolution of established discipline fluencies into new virtual, encompassing, networked vocabularies.

Australian Centre for the Moving Image (ACMI)'s engagement with this research project and the articulation of this practice into theory, which is contained in this book, provides for a strong foundational understanding of how games can move from the entertainment sector into the classroom as potent texts in their own right.

Much of the research and indeed many of the case studies found in this book underpin ACMI's position as an international centre that presents and champions the art and culture of the moving image in all its forms. We celebrate and explore film, television, videogames, art and digital culture through a vibrant range of exhibitions, screenings, events, workshops, collections and research resources. We foster ideas, talent and innovation, and inspire people of all kinds to experience and engage richly with screen culture as it evolves.

Through our programs and partnerships, like the ARC research found in this text, we bring excellence and innovation in international screen culture to Australia, and represent Australia's creative spirit and practice to the world. Whether presenting the masterpieces of world cinema or experimental artworks, showcasing emerging creative talent, or exploring the social impact of digital media, we provide rich opportunities to experience, engage with and contribute to how the moving image is changing our lives.

More critically the education research and practice within ACMI, which is reflected in the pages that follow, is about the synthesis of digital culture, and its translation to educational framework that acts as creative catalyst for learners to move beyond the realms of reader participants to the more active, experiential and innovative spaces inhabited by 21st century learners.

The Victorian Association for the Teaching of English

The Victorian Association for the Teaching of English (VATE) has a firmly held and long-standing commitment to a rich, inclusive understanding of literacy, in which young people's literacy is situated in its social and cultural context. VATE is vitally interested in the full range of literacy practices of young people, in particular the kinds of electronic literacy that have been the focus of this project.

VATE's involvement began in early 2006 when Catherine Beavis initially approached Council with the proposal that VATE become an industry partner. The response from Council was enthusiastic and supportive. Even then, many of VATE's members were still becoming familiar with the use of technology in teaching, and computer games were by and large a complete unknown. The prospect of joining in a forward-reaching project, exploring the potential for literacy learning through the use of gaming technology, was both exciting and a little daunting.

As with all things technological, changes are rapid and difficult to keep up with. The road travelled from that time until the present has had many twists and turns, and the journey has involved some surprises and not inconsiderable revelations. We are much more comfortable not only with the technology but also with the pace of change and with the imperative to keep up with, and to some extent provide, leadership in innovation and practice.

This book not only provides a model for teachers keen to understand how computer games can enhance literacy learning, but also illustrates the practical application of the theory in English classrooms through the various case studies presented. Equipped with this shared understanding and language, English educators can confidently engage with the 'brave new worlds' of computer game technology.

Louise Dressing, Department of Education and Early Childhood Development
Gael McIndoe, Australian Centre for the Moving Image
Debbie DeLaps, Victorian Association for the Teaching of English

Part 1

Framing chapters

Chapter 1

Literacy learning and computer games: A curriculum challenge for our times

Catherine Beavis, Joanne O'Mara and Lisa McNeice

This book comes from the work of many teachers, researchers and observant others who contributed to the three year project, *Literacy in the Digital World of the Twenty-first Century: Learning from Computer Games*. Like much work in education, when the project was first conceived, we did not imagine the shape of the final journey, the people we would encounter along the way and the relationships we would form with different teachers, schools, researchers and theorists as a result of this project. The book represents the work of the teachers, students, academics and educators who participated in the project, underpinned by the vision and contribution of the Industry Partners: The Department of Education and Early Childhood Development in Victoria, the Australian Centre for the Moving Image and the Victorian Association for the Teaching of English. It conveys a sense of our exploration, and maps the territory we covered and what individually and collectively participants in the project have realised. The project team comprised Catherine Beavis, Clare Bradford, Joanne O'Mara and Christopher S. Walsh, together with Research Fellow Thomas Apperley, and a team of teacher researchers including co-editor Lisa McNeice. Research assistance was provided by Amanda Gutierrez and Phillipa Hodder at Deakin University, and by Joy Reynolds and Jay Deagon at Griffith University. In conjunction with the Industry Partners, the project was funded by the Australian Research Council under its Linkage scheme.

Why computer games? Why in school?

There are two themes to which we have returned again and again in different guises throughout the life of the project. The first concerns the connection that many young people have with computer games or videogames, in their out-of-school worlds. Are there ways we might build bridges between in- and out-of-school worlds through recognising and incorporating many students' deep involvement with digital culture and their knowledge and expertise in negotiating the online world? Might we be able to draw on that knowledge, and the kinds of engagement, cooperation, problem solving and critique fostered by many popular computer games, to make school more 'relevant,' both in relation to how students see school and with respect to 'new' forms of knowledge and curriculum?

These questions raised a number of others. What might we learn about our students and contemporary literacy practices by observing their involvement with games in their leisure worlds? What might happen if we brought games into the classroom in different ways? How might we do so? Once these questions were raised, more followed. Are there skills that young people use in their gaming that might apply to schooling? Is this 'on the edge' activity really part of the mainstream? What might it mean for a teacher to use games in his or her classroom? How might students make and create their own games at school? Could learning at school be enlivened by the introduction of out-of-school knowledge and activities? Could games be more than just a motivational tool to spark interest in traditional curriculum activities?

The second theme focuses on the changing nature of literacy and what it might mean to be a 'literate person' now and in the future. Our work is based on our understanding that literacy is changing as a result of new technologies and that this has important implications for the English classroom. So we considered the ways in which and the extent to which games functioned as new forms of text and literacy. We wondered what young people were doing as they played games, what, if any, literacy skills they were developing and how 'games literacy' might be described. We observed that students were very agential in their relationships with games, both in the ways in which they played and when they were designing their own games or designing within the gameworld. There seemed to be a knowing and critical edge to the ways in which the students with whom we worked positioned themselves in relationship to their games and gaming that is often overlooked in popular discourse. Teachers in the project observed that students seemed highly engaged with the units of work they had designed around games, and that working with games opened up new spaces for conversation and relationships. In addition, for many students, new insights, skills and understandings in relation to print and/or digital literacies seemed to grow out of their use and/or analysis of games. This seemed to be worth pursuing.

In our initial planning for the project we drew on four sets or frameworks of ideas to think about games, young people and literacy. Traces of these frameworks can be seen in different ways in most of the chapters in the book. The first framework came from work in media and cultural studies that brought together institutions, texts and audiences, as seen, for example, in the work of David Buckingham (2000) and Julian Sefton-Green (1998). It came to include also more recent work from these writers (e.g., Buckingham, 2007; Sefton-Green, 2006) and other researchers in the fields of digital culture, new media, new literacies and participatory culture. These include such figures as Donna Alvermann (2010), Andrew Burn (2009), James Gee (2003), Henry Jenkins (2006) and Jackie Marsh (2005). This work provided a generative framework for understanding games as media texts, the social and creative energies entailed in gameplay, and the new and traditional literacy practices surrounding them.

A second framework came from sociological studies of the place of digital culture in young people's lives. This framework provided a way of understanding something of the functions and consequences of digital literacies in the lives of adolescents and their embeddedness in games culture and global marketing, together with their implications for school contexts and literacy education. Representative researchers here include Bourdieu & Wacquant (1992); Carrington & Luke (1997), researchers in the new social studies of childhood (e.g., Hutchby & Moran-Ellis, 2001) and social geographers such as Livingstone & Haddon (2009). As the project progressed, this framework came also to include work specific to the games studies, in particular Bogost's notion of 'procedural rhetoric' (2007), Galloway's (2006) emphasis on the role of the machine and Consalvo's notion of 'gaming capital' (2007).

We wanted to explore the ways in which games told stories, and to learn more about the ways in which new and traditional forms of narrative, positioning, representation and response were combined. We were also interested in games as new forms of communication, and the view of literacy as design. A third framework therefore drew together work from the fields of children's literature, digital culture, drama and semiotics, drawing on literary and play theory and grammars of visual design. Resources here included research by project member Clare Bradford (2006), and Kress & van Leeuwin's 'grammar of visual design' (1996).

The fourth framework, which helped us bring together the different strands of the project and to support the research, planning and teaching undertaken by teachers in the project was Green's 3D L(IT)eracy model (1999). This model, originally developed in relation to writing in the subject areas and further adapted to provide a way of 'thinking together' literacy and Information Technology (IT), argues the need to attend to 'cultural, critical and operational' dimensions in thinking about texts and literacy, and to incorporate all three dimensions in integrated ways in curriculum planning in English and other subject areas and in teaching with, through and about literacy (Durrant & Green, 2000, pp. 97–98). The three dimensions of this model – cultural, critical and operational – are all represented in these chapters in various ways. The model has been and continues to be influential in our thinking about how games might be used in classroom and what this might mean for teachers and schools.

Over the course of the project, a model for thinking about games and literacy was developed, arising from the work of the teachers, students and researchers, the initial theorisation through Green's 3D model and Games Studies perspectives introduced into the project by Tom Apperley. This model is presented in Chapter Two. It appears again later in the book where Tom and Catherine visit each of the school-based chapters, noting the areas that the chapters addressed, and discussing each chapter in terms of how the activities and approaches they describe sit with respect to the model. We hope that these chapters, and the model, will be useful resources for teachers and researchers engaging with work of this kind. In addition, we are indebted to Tom Apperley for the compilation of additional resources presented in Part 5.

Exploring, arriving and re-viewing

This work provides a variety of perspectives on games, literacy and learning. The research projects represented in this book were conducted in schools, and were reliant upon the partnerships and generosity of teachers. We are very pleased that so much of their work is represented here. One of the things we did not anticipate was the breadth of teacher research that would be undertaken and the different circumstances and approaches. These chapters explore a range of different approaches to games in English including creating games in the classroom, creating new texts from the games, analysing games and gameworlds as texts and exploring what it means to play games.

The three of us as co-editors have brought different experiences to the research project and this book. Catherine has been researching literacy and computer games since 1995. For her, the project was an opportunity to build on earlier work with teachers and students exploring English, literacy and computer games, and to work with a range of colleagues from different areas to investigate further the kinds of phenomena games are, the ways young people engage with them, and the implications for English and literacy. She writes:

> *For years I've been fascinated with the idea of computer games as 'texts'; with the ways playing games requires players to call on a wide range of knowledge and resources, including the capacity to simultaneously interpret and respond to an interacting set of multimodal forms of representation on the screen – sound, movement, colour, imagery, symbol, characters and so on – and with how games seemed to be pushing the boundaries of literacy and embodying new forms of narrative. I liked the idea of games as 'emergent cultural forms' – whatever that might mean – and I was impressed by the richness and complexity of many games. I could not help being struck by the high levels of skill, energy and commitment young players brought to the world of games, their participation in the games community and the care taken in many instances in managing the terms of that participation and their representation there.*
>
> *Thinking about all this in relation to English teaching and curriculum, it seemed to me that there were many questions and possibilities here: for students and teachers to learn more about the literacies and narrative forms of games; for connecting school curriculum and teaching with the world beyond school and for learning more about new literacies and multimodal literacies. It seemed there were opportunities here for critical examination and reflection and the development of critical literacy perspectives on games; and for learning more about learning – in particular, the collaborative problem-solving orientations often fostered by games, and the use of 'distributed knowledge.' It also seemed important to consider how attention to such matters articulated with the traditional concerns of English teaching and curriculum, and how they challenged or contributed to subject renewal for English in the digital world. The project offered the chance to explore questions such as these with a like-minded community 'on the ground.' It has been exciting and informative to learn from teachers*

and students in the project about how they see and negotiate matters such as these, and to work with colleagues from so many diverse areas to arrive at a rich (and not always comfortable or consistent) set of perspectives on what we might learn from games and students' engagement with them for 21st century English Curriculum and literacy.

Jo, having worked with Catherine from 2001 teaching English method at Deakin University, gradually became more and more interested in games through connecting with Catherine's research. She writes:

Having trained initially as an English and Media Studies teacher, I see these two disciplines as merging due to the changing nature of texts and literacy. Engaging with the 'outsiders' to school education with whom we worked in this project was intellectually invigorating and gave us new ways of seeing the work. Brett Mclennan and Vince Trundle from the Australian Centre for the Moving Image (ACMI) provided screen-based insights and analysis. Vince Trundle worked with Pip Hodder and myself, as we interviewed students from the different participating schools about how they were reading the screens when they were playing the games. The insightful questions Vince asked the students expanded my understanding of the enactment of screen semiotics – how these students were processing all the information with which they were working and then translating them into actions in the games. Tom Apperley brought an incredible depth of knowledge and respect for games and the cultural and critical theories that are being developed around gaming. This was significant for connecting the educational aspect of the work into the broader games field. Clare Bradford's narrative analysis was spectacular and challenging, and the importance of the changing nature of contemporary narratives to English Curriculum cannot be underestimated.

The teachers with whom we worked are represented in the book, with most of them contributing chapters. Members of the Deakin team worked in different schools, and got to know the work of participating teachers accordingly. Significant for me was the work John Richards did on game-making with his students. His approach to the classroom, the ways in which he structured the relationships with his students and the preparation these students are doing for their futures was stunning and has made me re-think the way relationships can be forged and supported in classrooms. I also worked with the drama teacher at his school, Belinda Lees, to further investigate the ways the students positioned themselves within the world of games, which was fun and revealing. I really enjoyed working with Jeannette Hannaford as she completed her Masters of Education degree. Her findings from an after-school computer club were unexpected and challenging. In addition to the work of classroom teachers, I found the ways in which the teacher-librarian developed his library-based program to extend and connect with his students outside of their regular classrooms exciting and practical.

As I continue to work with teachers in training and teachers in school, and watch my own children growing up with computer games, it is more and more obvious how important they are to our culture and the possibilities they hold for education.

Lisa, English coordinator at one of the project schools, was inspired to use computer games in the English classroom after seeing presentations from many members of the project team during the Australian Government Summer School for Teachers in 2008. She writes:

The Summer School included a trip to ACMI which brought on a realisation so startling in its simplicity I was ashamed that I'd never thought of it before. I already knew that our most fundamental task as teachers is to meet the students where they are ... where they are already actively literate, where they are already successfully communicating, where their identity is acknowledged and respected, and where they are already showing leadership, team work, curiosity and taking active creative control within a context. What I hadn't done was connect this to computer games in my teaching. Why not?

I suddenly had a vision of my Year 9 English class. Scenario: kids are happily playing computer games; I come in. 'Stop playing games!' I say. (Subtext: Stop communicating, stop seeking and absorbing information from multiple sources and synthesising that information so you can make decisions and act on those decisions. Stop having fun!) 'We're going to do English now!' Groans, reluctant but largely good-willed acquiescence, a withdrawing, a settling down, a glazing over.

What if I could change that scenario? What if my colleagues and I could create a unit of work that revelled in the students' exploration of computer games? That allowed us to say, 'Keep playing games! And tell us all about it!'

I was not a computer-game player, but I had a keen interest in games as text, and I worked from that starting point. As I worked with the project leaders and other participants, however, I came to see games as being as much (or more) to do with action as with text. The model for games and literacy developed through the project is helping me with my own journey towards the successful teaching of digital literacy in the 21st century. My design approach started from the relative safety of the idea of the text within the action. In future, though, I'll be moving much more towards exploring the digital literacy imperatives and possibilities provided by the action within the text.

Professor Claire Wyatt-Smith, Dean (Academic) for Arts, Education and Law at Griffith University said at a recent gathering of teachers, 'The agency of children in directing learning is forced on us in the realm of technology.' This is true, but in good teaching this has always been the case – or should have been. We must continue to acknowledge the agency of our students (that is, their authentic selves, their interests, their active realms where they feel acknowledged and articulate) in directing learning into the future.

Teachers know that students learn when they're having fun and being challenged. I learned a huge amount from this project.

In addition to the teachers and other writers included in this book, a number of key figures have been essential to the project's success in many ways. Louise Dressing, and through her the Department of Education and Early Childhood Development in Victoria, provided unfailing interest, presence and support in many ways. Her deep understanding of the realities of school and of teachers' and students' needs, and her ongoing commitment and openness to exploring new possibilities for curriculum and pedagogy to meet these needs, made her a central player. Gael McIndoe of the Australian Centre for the Moving Image (ACMI) saw the possibilities of the project from the earliest times, approved ACMI's participation, introduced us to Brett McLennan and Vincent Trundle, project stalwarts, and donated extensive time and usage of the ACMI facilities, including the ACMI games lab, and the 2008 *Game On!* exhibition of computer games. Days at the ACMI games lab under the guidance of Brett and Vincent provided much-needed 'games literacy' education for many of the teachers and researchers on the team, in addition to providing an invaluable location for the observation and analysis of students' gameplay. Greg Houghton, then President of VATE, together with the council at that time, saw the proposed project as consistent with VATE's long-standing commitment to a rich and inclusive understanding of literacy, in which young people's literacy is situated in its social and cultural context.

Since that time, Debbie De Laps, Executive officer of VATE, Kate Gillespie and Gemma Walsh have provided ongoing and practical support, in particular through their hospitality in hosting project professional learning days and in creating space for the presentation of teacher research and project outcomes in the annual conferences in 2008 and 2009. A further network of invisible but essential support was provided by Josephine Wee and Anne Brocklebank at Deakin University, and Sue Lau and Deb Brooks at Griffith University. Finally, the project could not have begun at all without the support of the participating schools: the principals, teachers, students, parents and jurisdictions involved. We offer them heart-felt thanks.

Chapter 2

A model for games and literacy

Catherine Beavis and Thomas Apperley

Introduction

English Curriculum today, in Australia as elsewhere, is built on a view of literacy that encompasses but extends beyond traditional print and oral forms to include the digital, multimodal forms of text and literacy brought about through Information and Communication Technologies. The Australian Curriculum: English, for example, aims to ensure that students:

> *learn to listen to, read, view, speak, write, create and reflect on increasingly complex and sophisticated spoken, written and multimodal texts across a growing range of contexts with accuracy, fluency and purpose.* (Australian Curriculum Assessment and Reporting Authority [ACARA], 2010)

Curriculum and teaching that combines literacy and technology needs to help students become capable, critical and creative in both print and digital forms. To do so, however, it needs to go beyond teaching mastery of print forms to develop fuller understandings and capabilities in digital texts and literacies. This requires a way of thinking about multimodal forms of text and literacy that is not framed by assumptions about print and verbal forms, but, rather, recognises the particular qualities or 'affordances' of multimodal forms, and starts from there.

In this project, we set out to learn more about how to think about and understand the cultural artefacts variously called 'computer games,' 'videogames' or 'digital games' from the point of view of English and literacy curriculum and teaching. Computer games, as popular, complex and sophisticated examples of digital culture, are an important part of many students' lives. They are also an important context for many students for a wide range of meaning-making and communicative activity. A central challenge for teachers in the project in planning curriculum around computer games was how to combine perspectives from the standpoint of English Curriculum on the one hand, with its traditional concerns with text and literacy, with the very different contexts, skills and operations entailed in playing computer games. How should we understand computer games, and the practices and actions entailed in playing? Should we think about games as text, or think of them more in terms of action? In this chapter, we discuss digital games from both points of view – as action and as text. We outline key elements and arguments from each perspective, and present a model that combines both views, as a framework for curriculum planning.

A crucial foundational concept in game studies that is useful for bringing together the two perspectives is the notion of 'ergodic' (Aarseth, 1997). The key idea here is that the 'text' of digital games is produced through the interactions of the game (software and hardware) and the player, or players. By introducing the term 'ergodic' Aarseth underscores the physical role of the player in the configuration of the final game 'text.' Players do not shift between ergodic and textual modes, rather these modes intertwine and feedback into each other (Bogost, 2006).

Digital gaming is associated with the development of a large number of more or less tangible skills. This is to suggest not that some skills have less robust connections to gameplay, but that the skills are developed indirectly, rather than learned in-game through the process of play. Players can 'develop 21st century skills in a spontaneous and holistic way as a by-product of play' (Galarneau & Zibit, 2007, p. 61). Galarneau and Zibit also highlight the importance of digital game in fostering particular *attitudes* towards learning, organising, knowledge sharing, and collaboration. This suggests that the significance of inclusion in digital gameplay and cultures is palpable.

For us, digital games present a particularly important and interesting challenge for literacy and English teachers and curriculum.[1] Digital games deserve a central place as part of an expanded repertoire of texts brought into the

---

1 We use the term 'digital games' to cover all games played on a rapidly expanding variety of platforms including computers, consoles, and mobile and handheld devices.

curriculum for study, but they should not be understood simply in textual terms. While games' 'meanings' are negotiated and produced in the interaction between 'text' and reader, as is the case with any text, it is important to understand how they are enacted and instantiated through *action* (Galloway, 2006). The nature of games as both text and action implies the need for a multilayered way of thinking about games literacy in the classroom.

In this chapter, we propose a model for the classroom study of digital games that brings together these two separate but related perspectives: one concerned with games and gameplay as text, and one as action. Understanding games, and reconceptualising curriculum to capitalise on the possibilities and affordances to support learning offered by digital games, has great potential to build strong bridges between the life-worlds of students out of school, and 21st century curriculum. However, in order to understand students' gaming practices, some effort must be undertaken to understand digital games on their own terms. The model that we introduce responds to this undertaking by both recognising the distinctiveness of digital games as cultural phenomena, and demonstrating how this uniqueness may be situated alongside contemporary understandings of literacy and multimodal literacy practices. The model is represented as a pinwheel, with the two layers, games as text and games as action, moving freely and independently, with different alignments between layers at different times, but the two layers always understood as working together.

A model for games literacy

Perspective one: Games as action

Actions

The notion of action marks a key difference between digital games and other media forms. Actions define both the characters – in terms of the type and variety of actions that the avatar can perform – and the virtual spaces of the digital games, because actions define *how* the space(s), and the objects in it, will be used by the players. Galloway's (2006) concept of action as central to how games are played extends to examine the dynamic of inter*action* between the player and the computer.

Digital games are enacted at two levels: by the players and by the console that reads and activates the games' source data. The digital game comes into being through the feedback relations between actions taken by the player(s) and the game (Galloway, 2006, p. 4). This distinction is extremely useful because it draws out a critical distinction between what the player does and what the computer does in what might be otherwise understood as an amorphous, homogenous, and unspecific session of gameplay. It allows for closer focus on the choices players make and the ways they respond to what they see, and a clearer sense of *how* they are contributing to the creation of the game. Furthermore, the notion of action highlights how different games and game genres require specific approaches that incorporate particular forms of knowledge, both of the genre and its conventions, and of how actions are performed. For example, the player must recognise how their avatar moves, and the actions it can perform (e.g., kick, jump, shoot), and know how to execute these actions rapidly and at will.

Design
Design embraces several crucial and related meanings: the combination of elements of production within digital games that players encounter and with which they interact during the course of play; the process of multimodal meaning-making and design that is involved in re-presenting and recontextualising game information through the creation of texts deriving from the game – what Consalvo (2007) calls 'paratexts'; and the process of redesigning games. Design thus provides a concept that links the creation, reading and use of (para)texts with play and game design.

A common feature among recent and contemporary digital games today is allowing the players some degree of control over design elements of the game. This does not mean that they build the game from the ground up, but rather that they can make decisions that changes how the game will be played, and thus may shape the game. Many of these design choices are largely aesthetic, but the ability to customise areas of the game-world is an increasingly common feature, and may include elements of design that impact on how the game is played.

Situation(s)
The situation of play refers primarily to its context. While emphasis is often given to the virtual elements of play, it is also important to think about the spaces in which digital games are enacted (Stevens, Satwicz, & McCarthy, 2008). Examining gameplay in this context emphasises the learning and

Digital games: Literacy in action

sociality that takes place during the experience of gaming, and how gaming is connected with – and a part of – other mundane daily activities (Apperley, 2010). An awareness of the importance and effect of context on how games are played is consistent with insights familiar in English and literacy education about the socially situated nature of literacy and related activities, and the ways in which environment shapes meaning and purpose. An awareness of the importance of situation is particularly useful for teachers and researchers interested in understanding how literacies develop in out-of-school environments, and what might be learnt from these to take back into the classroom more formally.

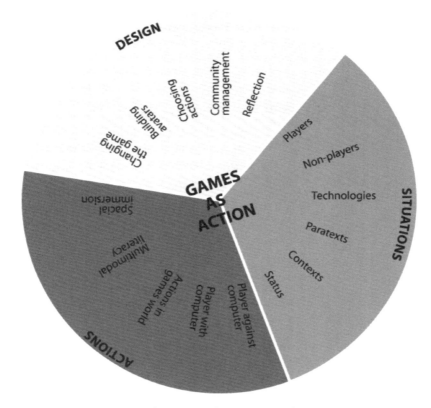

Figure 2.1 Games as action

When digital games are played, people and technologies are working together in many different ways. At least one person is playing. Other players could be playing from different locations over a network, or in the same room. Often a group will play, taking turns to play and watch others play. Despite the competitive focus of many multiplayer games, there is considerable cooperation in the ways in which situation, knowledge and information are shared. Players learn from one another both directly and indirectly through the exchange of 'gaming capital' and in other ways (Consalvo, 2007; Walsh & Apperley, 2009, Beavis, Nixon & Atkinson, 2005).

These three dimensions – actions, design and situation(s) – organise this layer of the model, in an overlapping and mutually constitutive relationship with each other.

The action layer of the model can thus be represented in this way (see Figure 2.1 Games as action, above).

Perspective two: Games as text

The Games as text layer maps four dimensions of study in relation to the central focus on gameplay. This layer overlaps and intersects with the Games as action layer, but provides for a different orientation aligned more closely with traditional priorities related to texts and literacies in the English/Literacy classroom. The starting point for this view of games and their study as textual forms derives from the approach to language education historically familiar to English and literacy educators: learning language, learning through language and learning about language (Halliday, 1980). The four dimensions in this layer focus on:

- Knowledge about games
- The world around the game
- Me as games player
- Learning through games.

While one dimension is likely to be emphasised over the others in any given unit of work, the dimensions are not discrete, but rather mutually informing and informed, so that elements from different dimensions may be drawn in to study at any time. The dimensions might better be thought of as lenses or vectors, with the game and gameplay reciprocally illuminating and being illuminated by the dimension or lens brought to bear. The active experience of play sits at the model's heart.

The Games as text layer of the model might be represented in this way (see Figure 2.2 Games as text):

Knowledge about games

This dimension examines games as cultural artefacts, with attention to narrative and aesthetic aspects, and includes critical literacy perspectives on games

Digital games: Literacy in action

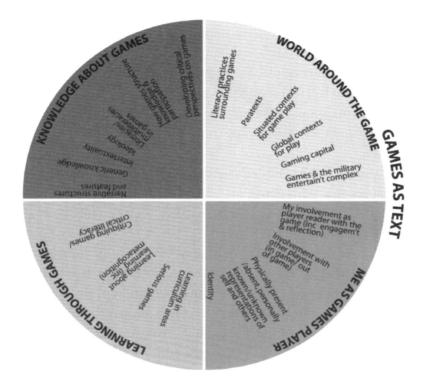

Figure 2.2 Games as text

and gameplay. It considers the role of generic and intertextual knowledge in informing understandings and gameplay. For example, students might study narrative structures and features of specific games, and their relation to other narratives in games and other modes, and call on or develop their knowledge of the characteristics and features of the relevant genre, looking at how, in this instance, those generic features have been used, and to what effect.

Me as games player

This dimension focuses on reflexivity about students as games players, including issues of value, ideology, and identity and the ways players are positioned by the game. This provides the opportunity to explore issues related to students' involvement with the game as player/creator/'reader' and a focus on engagement and reflection. Work in this dimension is closely linked to the focus on games as 'cultural artefacts,' and on the world around the game. It includes analysis of how the player is positioned by the game and how they take up or resist that positioning. This consideration of play with known and unknown others can springboard into an examination of representations of self and others, of how these representations are constructed and interpreted, through visual means but also through values, voice and competencies as revealed through play.

The world around the game
The primary focus of this dimension is the broader local and global contexts in which games and gameplay take place. Foci include discussion of a range of contexts for play, including physical and virtual spaces, public and private locations, and settings shared with others or experienced alone. It also considers how that situatedness and those relationships construct and affect the experience of gameplay.

Learning through games
This dimension examines the capacity of games to teach or impart information through what Bogost (2007) calls procedural rhetoric – the ways in which players learn or take on a particular understanding or perspective through following the logic of the game through play. This logic is somewhat analogous to the way learning takes place through process drama. It includes game-supported learning in curriculum areas, both through games specifically designed for use in disciplinary domains, and the use of commercial, off-the-shelf games. It includes increased awareness of metacognitive strategies and processes, and the development of critical perspectives on both games and the social issues and problems they illuminate.

Bringing the two together
What does this look like in practice, in teaching terms? Bringing both layers of the model together, in relation to curriculum and teaching, foregrounds the following elements (see Table 2.1 Games as action and games as text)

In thinking about games and literacy together in the way we propose, there are clear commonalities, links and overlaps that exist between the two layers. Each layer, however, also works individually. In both layers the constituent elements or dimensions are integrally related to each other, so that both within and between the layers the categories we introduce need to be conceived as mutually influential. The changing and dynamic nature of the relationships and overlap between layers, and the categories within them might be better represented as follows, where the two layers of the pinwheel are conceived of as moveable and in play.

Table 2.1 Games as action and games as text

Games as action	Games as text
Curriculum design and teaching to foreground	
Situation(s) • Players • Non players • Technologies • Paratexts • Contexts • Status **Design** • Changing the game • Building avatars • Choosing actions • Building objects • Community management • Reflection **Actions** • Player against computer • Player with computer • Actions in games world • Multimodal literacy • Spatial immersion	**Knowledge about games** • Narrative structures and features • Generic knowledge • Intertextuality • Ideology • Literacies/multiliteracies in games • How games structure knowledge and participation • Developing critical perspectives on games **The world around the game** • Situated contexts for gameplay • Paratexts • Literacy practices surrounding games • Global contexts for play • Gaming capital • Games and the military/ entertainment complex **Me as games player** • Involvement as player/reader (including engagement and reflection) • Involvement with other players (in game/out of game) • Physically present/absent, personally known/unknown (includes representation of self and others) • Identity **Learning through games** • Learning in curriculum areas • Serious games • Learning about learning (including metacognition) • Critiquing games/critical literacy

The model is intended to provide a framework for planning games-based curriculum and pedagogy, and arises from a mapping of characteristic features of digital games and gameplay. A number of elements are held in common. Key concepts across both layers are context, situatedness and design. The importance of context and purpose in language learning and the role of context in shaping the construction of meaning have long been central tenets of English and literacy curriculum theory. Similarly, the view of literacy as socially situated practice is well established in New Literacies scholarship on reading, speaking and writing (e.g., Barton, Hamilton, & Ivanic, 2000) and on new media and digital culture (e.g., Lankshear & Knobel, 2007). Our

A model for games and literacy

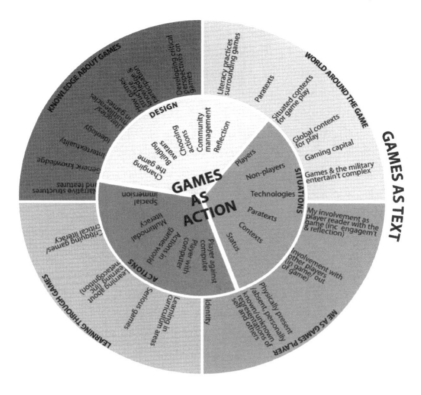

Figure 2.3 Games as action, games as text: curriculum and teaching dimensions

work and that of others on literacy and computer games has been posited on this understanding (e.g., Beavis, 2007; Gee, 2003).

Design is a familiar term in the theorisation of multimodal literacy (New London Group, 1996; Kress, 2003). In the model we propose, design embraces a number of crucial and related meanings and bridges across both layers, related to digital games conceived both primarily in terms of text, and primarily in terms of action. The synthesis provided by Gee (2003, p. 49) between literacy and digital games foregrounds the centrality of design in both fields. As he puts it, '[in playing games] learning about and coming to appreciate design and design principles is core to the learning experience.' Similarly, 'Learning about and coming to appreciate interrelations within and across multiple sign systems (images, words, actions, symbols, artefacts etc.) as a complex system is core to the learning experience' (2003, p. 49). As a term, 'design' is both noun and verb; it describes the relationship between meaning-making elements on a screen or page, and action – the process of designing as a creative activity, with multimodal literacy reconceptualised as 'design.'

Yet there are important differences too. Key amongst them is the recognition, in layer one, of those aspects outside a player's control and the active role played by the machine, the algorithms and other elements of gameplay. Layer one maps dimensions of play almost ethnographically, observing the interrelationships in how games are played. This mapping provides a guide for developing curriculum that mirrors the out-of-school nature of gameplay. Layer one insists strongly that games should not be conceived of in primarily textual ways. Layer two, by contrast, not only differs in its text-based take on games, it also works in a more prescriptive fashion to provide a template for curriculum planning and pedagogy that foregrounds the study of games within English curricula to support both traditional and new literacies.

This model for games literacy (games as text, games as action) arose from the team's reading of what the research says about games and about literacy, from discussions with the project teachers, and from our observations of the classroom units they developed and taught using games in their classrooms. It is our view that both layers of the model are essential, and that they speak to each other in multiple ways. Different contexts, different classrooms, different students and different curriculum mandates will result in the model being used in various ways. What is essential is that curriculum designed around digital games reflects and respects the nature of games, the nature of gameplay, and the integrity and experience of young people as games players.

To show how the model works in practice, and how it might operate as a guide for curriculum planning, at the ends of Chapters 3–12 we comment on how the units each chapter describes work in relation to the two layers of the model. We note how the units utilise concepts of games that correspond to games viewed as both text and action in connecting students' experience of this form of digital culture and new and traditional forms of literacy with curriculum in English and other subject areas. We comment briefly on each unit to show the kinds of activities and foci that different layers and dimensions of the model foreground, to show what the model looks like in practice, and to explore how the model might help with resources, planning and pedagogy in curriculum addressing games and literacy. In many instances, the discussion foregrounds ways in which elements of both layers overlap and intersect. The chapters present prototypes and possibilities for developing deeper and more complex understandings of both new and traditional literacies and of these digital cultural artefacts of the contemporary world.

Part 2

Perspectives from the classroom

Chapter 3

Computer games, archetypes and the quest narrative: Computer games as texts in the Year 9 English classroom

Lisa McNeice, Andrea Smith and Toby Robison

Overview of chapter

The main goal of this games unit was to allow students to develop their critical literacy skills within a context that was personally relevant to them. We started with a focus on J.R.R. Tolkien's use of archetypes and the quest narrative in his novel *The Fellowship of the Ring*. We encouraged students to analyse a narrative-based computer game of their choice; and to design a computer game of their own using these text elements. We hoped to encourage students to examine critically how games designers transgress, replicate or challenge the quest narrative, archetypes and stereotypes. It was hoped that by recognising and identifying these textual features, students would gain a greater understanding of the texts' cultural foundations, whilst questioning how they shape our sense of identity and world perspectives. We also hoped that students would reflect on the nature of gaming itself and embrace the chance to contribute to current debates around gaming.

Digital learners – Inspiration and justification for the unit

Our journey started in January 2008 with a visit to the Australian Centre for the Moving Image (ACMI) where Brett McLennan asked a group of secondary teachers, 'So, what's the 'problem' with new learners?' He suggested that there was no problem with the learners; there may, however, be a problem with our methods of engaging these learners. He encouraged the audience to picture this generation of students as being capable of dynamic immersion and innovative and creative activities – a generation who prefers immediate feedback, the opportunity to debate, and activities that engage with and/or use technology. We are dealing with the 'fast food, MTV generation'; active learners who thrive in a democratic learning environment where tasks and expectations are clearly defined, where they can challenge and question assumptions, and where teamwork and dialogue are valued. Students of the digital age are empowered, active, creative learners, not sponges.

As McLennan noted that day, our students are exposed to a vast array of communication fields, including television programs and commercials, videogames, mobile phone conversations, social networking sites, blogs and chat rooms. In their own fields and domains, where they have agency and the chance to be creative, members of the digital generation are very articulate, lucid and fluent. But, as McLennan pointed out, school is seen as an impediment to engagement via these forms. 'Why can't I have my mobile phone in class?' such a student could reasonably ask. 'It's how I communicate.' So, contrary to commonly held beliefs, we are dealing with a socially communicative generation rather than a collection of monosyllabic teens. Maybe they are not necessarily communicating in the traditional face-to-face scenarios, but they *are* communicating.

Our visit to ACMI inspired us to explore and seek new opportunities to engage students in an area where they are already using language to communicate actively and effectively. We realised the onus was on us to meet and engage with the students within this world, providing them with the critical literacy skills required to navigate it.

The steps – designing the unit

As the Year 9 English teaching team, we discussed the ideas contained in McLennan's presentation and their implications for us. We undertook readings and research related to the topic, focusing on James Paul Gee's *What video games have to teach us about learning and literacy* (Gee, 2003). We agreed we were keen to trial narrative computer games as part of the Year 9 text list and went on to create and implement a unit of work exploring computer games as texts. As a laptop school, we could ask each student to bring his or her own game to play for the duration of the unit, specifying only that it must be age-appropriate and narrative based.

Before moving on to unit design, the teachers gathered to play the games (often blindly with no game-based experience outside of *Pong!*) and create a list of suggested narrative-based computer games. This was a process that we found challenging, engaging, and, at times, downright hilarious. It led to many frustrated teachers being locked in digital rooms or pods within spaceships, unable to progress through the most basic level. We also discovered that it was often the most unexpected game, such as *Desperate Housewives*, that became a hit with teachers usually more comfortable with Austen or Shakespeare. In order to meet the aims of our unit, we had to find games with strong narratives that employed archetypal characters and a clear quest scenario. Effective games for the purposes of this unit fell into two categories. The first included those based on existing texts, including mystery/adventure games such as *Sherlock Holmes*, *Nancy Drew*, *Law and Order* and *CSI*, or fantasy/adventure games based on *Lord of the Rings*, *Harry Potter* and *Star Wars*. Titles created specifically for the medium, with easily accessible narratives and clearly identifiable archetypal characters, such as *Halo, The Elder Scrolls IV: Oblivion, Half Life 2* and *Assassin's Creed,* were also highly successful.

Previously, the students had studied archetypes in a unit of work designed by Joel Roache, one of the Year 9 English teachers (see Figure 3.1 and Figure 3.2). They had also examined the stages of the quest narrative (Figure 3.3), and were asked to apply the knowledge gained from both to a text already on the Year 9 booklist – Tolkien's *The Fellowship of the Ring*. Students read and discussed selected passages and watched the film version, while also investigating the wider use of archetypes and the quest narrative in print media and film. Lastly, as an introduction to our computer games unit, we took all our Year 9 students to ACMI's '*Game On*' exhibition.

- **The Fool** – the individual beginning a journey of self-discovery, often naive and in need of support and direction.
- **The Magician** – the Fool's guide on their journey, both inner and outer, often via an indirect route.
- **The High Priestess** – the Fool's guide into the hidden and dark realms of intuition and destiny to be found in the unconscious.
- **The Anima/Animus** – the Fool's feminine or masculine nature, often embodied in another, creating a balance of opposites.
- **The Hero** – representation of the Fool's powerful, courageous and strong aspects, as well as their destructive vanity, pride and ego.
- **The Shadow** – the Fool's dark nature, often projected out into the world in the form of another, usually extreme, form.

Figure 3.1 Common archetypes in literature and film

Computer games, archetypes and the quest narrative: Computer games as texts

The Fool

The Fool represents each of us as we begin something new in our lives, a journey, an adventure, or a new phase in our personal life. Archetypally, the Fool is most often the central character of a film or story. They begin the journey, discovering more about themselves and life in the process. Other characters in the story can often be seen as personifications of aspects of the Fool, for example, their courageous side, their feminine or masculine sides or their dark side. The Fool is not stupid, just naive as the journey begins, becoming more knowing as the journey moves to its conclusion.

Figure 3.2 The Fool from the unit on archetypes designed by Joel Roache

1. The Ordinary World
2. The Call to Adventure
3. Refusal of the Call
4. Meeting with the Mentor
5. Crossing the First Threshold
6. Tests, Allies, and Enemies
7. The Approach to the Inmost Cave
8. The Supreme Ordeal
9. Reward
10. The Road Back
11. Resurrection
12. Return with the Elixir

Figure 3.3 Stages in the quest narrative
Adapted from Joseph Campbell by Christopher Vogler, a Hollywood script consultant

The tasks

Task 1: Exploring digital worlds

In this task, students examined and reported their findings on two narrative-based computer games. They covered narrative, characters, setting and aims, whilst exploring how game designers chose to employ, exclude or transgress archetypal characters and the quest narrative. Students reflected on and wrote about the differences between print texts and digital texts, commenting on their similarities and differences.

After investigating their own digital text, students interviewed a classmate about their (different) game, examining essential elements such as setting and plot and the use of archetypes and the quest narrative. Students finished their report with a compare/contrast section where they explored how the digital worlds they examined differed from the world J.R.R. Tolkien created in his novel *The Fellowship of the Ring*. The students examined how the texts were different or alike and commented on the devices each creator used to construct their world (Figure 3.4).

> 'In the game, there are only a few characters that portray any archetypes. Altair is both the hero and the fool, because during the game, he kills a few to save many, making him a hero, but he learns much and is enlightened to how things really are in the world.
> Al Mualim is probably the only other character portraying major archetypes. He is both the magician and the shadow. At the start and for the majority of the game he is the one who helps you learn and improves your skills and knowledge. But at the end of the game you discover that he is in fact on the side of bad and evil, making him the shadow.
> Also in the story there is a relatively strong quest narrative, although what really must be done during the game is often hazy and hard to understand. The main part of the quest is killing all the bad leaders who are doing terrible things for what appears to be a greater good, but is in fact mainly for personal gain, as well as gaining your rank back. Then there are the many smaller, less significant parts of the quest, such as saving citizens and retrieving information from people.'

Figure 3.4 Extract from a student response to the task 'Exploring Digital Worlds'

Task 2: The essay

Students used the notes from their reports to write an essay. The strength of this task was that we could help the students focus on essay structure and expression, as they had already undertaken the research and had their findings at the ready.

Topics:

- Compare and contrast the use of archetypes in *The Fellowship of the Ring* and ONE selected computer game. What purpose do archetypes serve in telling those stories?

OR

- Compare and contrast the depiction of the quest narrative in *The Fellowship of the Ring* and ONE selected computer game. Which elements of the quest narrative do the storytellers use? Which do they discard? What is the effect?

Task 3: Pitching a game concept

In this task, the students used their choice of PowerPoint, web page, Word document, or brochure to present a 'pitch' for a new computer game to a panel of judges. The students had to come up with an idea for a computer game and then 'pitch' this idea to an audience in an effort to secure funding to develop their game. Presentations had to cover the narrative or plot of the game, an explanation of how the player is involved in the game and a description of the major characters in the form of physical and psychological profiles. Emphasis was placed on the effect of decisions on the part of the player and multiple narrative possibilities.

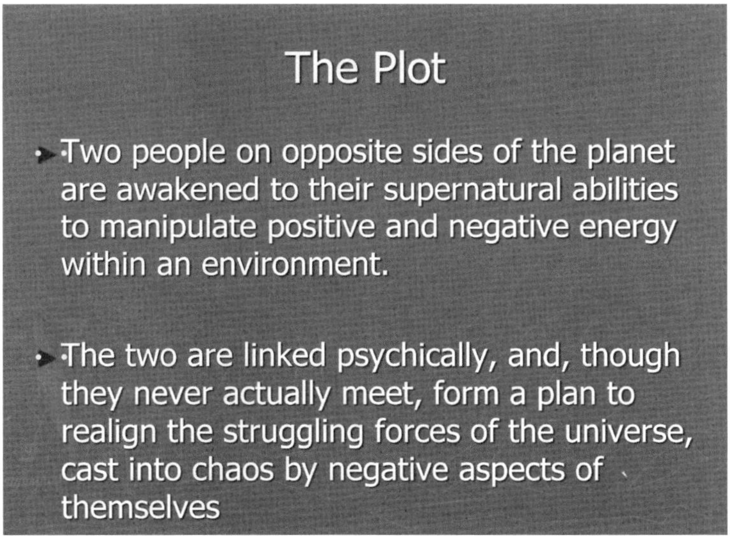

> **The Plot**
>
> - Two people on opposite sides of the planet are awakened to their supernatural abilities to manipulate positive and negative energy within an environment.
>
> - The two are linked psychically, and, though they never actually meet, form a plan to realign the struggling forces of the universe, cast into chaos by negative aspects of themselves

Figure 3.5 Excerpt from a student response to the task 'Pitching a Game Concept'

Task 4: The end-of-term extended response

Finally, the students wrote a reflective, research-based extended piece in response to the topic 'Parents! Are computer games bad for your children?'

FRIDAY, AUGUST 21, 2009 THE AGE
theage.com.au

Teen gamers at risk of gambling addiction

Jonathon Dart & Peter Hawkins

TEENAGERS who play video games regularly are more likely to develop the obsessive and anti-social tendencies that lead to problem gambling.

Researchers at the University of Adelaide surveyed 2669 teenagers aged between 13 and 17, and found that 56 per cent had gambled in the past year and 2.4 per cent had already become pathological gamblers, even before they turned 18.

That is higher than the 2.1 per cent of adults found to be problem gamblers by the Productivity Commission in 1999, although the level of harm, such as losing a house or a relationship, is much lower for adolescents.

The paper, due to be published in the Journal of Gambling Studies next month, found that teenage problem gamblers played arcade games three times more often than non-gamblers, and on average played hand-held games and internet games more than twice as often.

One of its authors, Associate Professor Paul Delfabbro, said teenage boys were more likely to play video games and gamble regularly, which is one reason for the correlation.

"The other reason is that the sorts of kids who are playing video games probably do so because they've got less parental supervision, they're probably bored, they probably don't have a lot of structured activity in their life," he said. "So the physical act of playing video games doesn't increase the risk of gambling but it is indicative

The Sydney Morning Herald smh.com.au May 28, 2008

Game girls

Girl gamers are on the rise, so why isn't anything being made for them? **Jason Hill** reports.

Wander into any videogame store and you could be forgiven for thinking that women do not play games at all but the statistics paint a different picture. More than 40% of gameplayers in Australia are female, yet most games on the store shelves are of little interest to them.

Despite this, the profile of the typical gamer has changed drastically over the past decade, with middle-aged housewives now as likely to play games as teenage boys. The average gamer in Australia is now 28 years old, up from 24 just two years ago. And despite being largely ignored by the game industry, 41% are female.

Women and older Australians are the fastest-growing audience for computer and video games and if trends continue, by 2014 the average age of Australian gamers will be the same as non-players - 42 - with an equal number of male and female players.

Trends are similar in the US, where 38% of gamers are female, spending an average 7.4 hours a week playing, according to the Entertainment Software Association.

ScienceDaily
Your source for the latest research news

News | Articles | Videos | Images | Books

Health & Medicine | Mind & Brain | Plants & Animals | Earth & Climate | Space & Time | Matter &

Science News

Blog | Cite

Video Game Players Love The Game, Not The Gore

ScienceDaily (Jan. 16, 2009) — The next time a loved one brandishes a virtual shotgun in their favorite video game, take heart. That look of glee, says a new study, likely stems from the healthy pleasure of mastering a challenge rather than from a disturbing craving for carnage.

Research to be published online January 16 in the Personality and Social Psychology Bulletin shows that, contrary to popular belief, violence does not make video games more enjoyable. The study by investigators at the University of Rochester and Immersyve Inc., a player-experience research firm, found that for many people, gore actually detracts from a game's "fun factor," decreasing players' interest and desire to purchase a game. When designing the next generation of video games, added the authors, developers should remember: blood does not help the bottom line.

"For the vast majority of players, even those who regularly play and enjoy violent games, violence was not a plus," explained Andrew Przybylski, a University graduate student and lead author of the study. "Violent content was only preferred by a small subgroup of people that generally report being more aggressive," added Przybylski, however, even these hostile players did not report increased pleasure when playing more gruesome games.

See Also:

Mind & Brain
- Anger Management
- PTSD

Computers & Math
- Video Games
- Artificial Intelligence

Science & Society
- Popular Culture
- Conflict

Living Well

Strange Science

Reference
- Massively multiplayer online game
- Experimental economics
- Computer and video game genres
- Application software

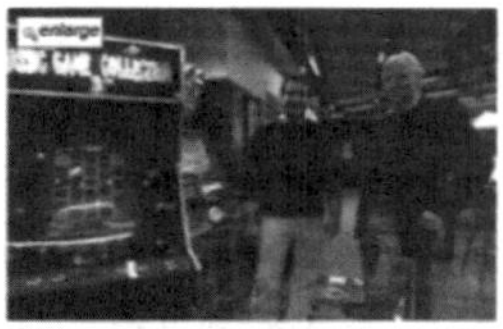

This is Scott Rigby (left) and Richard Ryan. (Credit: University of Rochester)

Related Stories

Figure 3.6 Extracts from the articles students used in their research for 'Parents! Are Computer Games Bad for Your Children?'

We provided several articles that supported computer games, and several that were quite damning of them (Figure 3.6). Students were expected to find further articles and create a bibliography to accompany their finished response. We found that the students felt very empowered, well-informed and keen to offer their opinions in response to this task.

All in all, we were surprised to find that the students produced more writing and wrote more willingly in response to this unit of work than in any other unit in Year 9. The students were in the position to 'teach their teachers,' and they really rose to the challenge.

Where to from here?

Our 'Computer Games as Texts' unit took 10 weeks to complete. It could easily be extended to a semester-length unit of work, with further research and assessment tasks being added to the study. Areas we thought we would like to explore further included the language of gaming (creating a glossary and commentary); the history of games and gaming; the ethical and social implications of videogames, including notions of communication, isolation and addiction; and the broader cultural aspect of gaming and its place in our society.

Games as text, games as action: the model as applied in this chapter

The teachers involved in this project created a curriculum unit that effectively developed students' understanding of literary features and conventions by exploring the ways in which elements familiar from film, myth and literature were taken up and used in the context of digital games. With respect to the **games as action** layer, the unit focused particularly on design. Task three, the pitching of a digital game, allowed students to use their knowledge to explore game *design* by presenting their vision for an imaginary game that a commercial game maker might take up and develop further. The task required the students to demonstrate their knowledge of the narrative conventions shared by digital games and literature. It also required pupils to contextualise this knowledge against the generic and structural conventions of digital games and thus show their proficiency in game *design*. With respect to **games** conceptualised **as text**, the unit focused particularly on *knowledge about games*, and provided contexts for students to develop their understandings of specific genres, and of narrative structures and features. Knowledge gained through the unit related to the role of these features, particularly characterisation, archetypes and plot in constructing narratives, and the ways in which these are created differently and the same through different media.

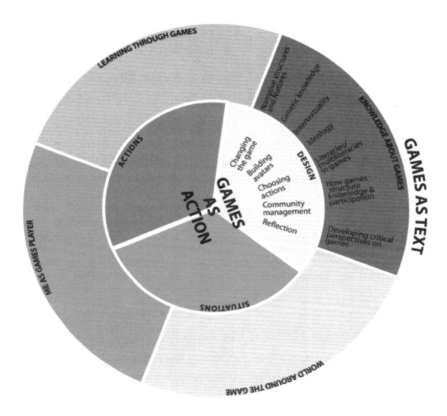

Figure 3.7 Games as text, games as action: Computer games, archetypes and the quest narrative

Chapter 4

Breaking through the fourth wall: Invitation from an avatar

Joanne O'Mara and Belinda Lees

Overview of chapter
This chapter reports how Year 8 boys described and understood the characters in their videogames, their analysis of how the game narratives were constructed, and how realistic (or not) these characters might be to them. Beginning with a focus-group discussion of videogame characters, we developed some drama work with the students to enable them to explore their ideas further. In this chapter the boys' responses are described and interpreted via interview data and teacher observations. The work clearly shows the high level of awareness that these students have about how they are positioned in the game and by society as young male gameplayers, and they actively subvert and play with these stereotypes in their drama work.

Playing around gaming
Young people are often positioned as lacking agency in their consumption of computer games and as victims of mass consumerism. The Year 8 students at this school all showed a strong sense of personal efficacy and autonomy, as they had already made their own games using *GameMaker* in Multimedia (see Chapter 7) and understood some of the intricacies of game design and production and marketing. In interviews with students who had made their own games, Jo had been struck by the boys' high level of cultural awareness about how computer games were portrayed in the media, and the general moral panic that surrounded their usage.

The drama workshop was designed to co-construct with the students some creative data about their understandings of games and to enable them to playfully explore some of the issues around the place of computer games in their lives. The workshop provided creative opportunities to extend their ideas into a range of 'what if ...' speculations. We were particularly interested in:

- Their perceptions of the real world as opposed to the gaming world
- Their perceptions of their parents' fears and insecurities relating to their hobby as a gamer
- Their perceptions and experiences of the virtual worlds, and whether there is any distortion of 'reality' when they re-enter the non-virtual world

Drama and other art forms are often used as qualitative research methodologies, and it is established that the creative arts enable participants to reliably express their ideas and feelings in different ways, rather than directly answering interview questions. We set up this workshop based on some of the questions the boys had been asked in focus-group interviews to enable these students to explore their answers in a creative way. Six students were identified by Belinda (who taught the boys Drama) from within the entire Year 8 cohort for their notable expressive skills and ability to work as effective team members, and these students were invited to participate in the drama workshop.

An invitation from an avatar

We wanted to set the tone of the workshop as fun, adventurous, creative, enquiring, exploratory and playful. Therefore, Belinda wrote an invitation from Gordon Freeman, who holds the enigmatic title of Theoretical Physicist at the Black Mesa Research Facility in the *Half Life* series. By distancing herself from the 'Drama teacher,' she hoped to tacitly communicate that the workshop would be entirely about the boys' experiences in their virtual worlds. This strategy seemed to carry more mystique than 'remember Ms Lees wants you to meet at recess to discuss the drama workshop that's on tomorrow.' More importantly, the invitation served as a pre-text for the drama workshop. O'Neill (1995) describes drama pre-texts as performing the dual functions of activating the weaving of the text of the drama process; and indicating that it exists prior to the drama as well as being the excuse or reason for the drama. The invitation from Dr Freeman (Figure 4.1) performed

Breaking through the fourth wall: Invitation from an avatar

all of these functions in our dramatic world, as well as giving the boys a sense that the session would be playful.

> FROM: DR GORDON FREEMAN (PhD MIT)
> You are to transcend the boundary between reality and virtual reality; to create and experience your ideal life in AVATAR LAND.
> MEET: WIL007, (Ms Lees' office), where you will receive secret location details
> DATE: 28 November
> TIME: 1100 hours EST
> CONTACT: Dr Gordon Freeman, via Ms Lees
> WARNING: Applicants are warned this is a scientific experiment, and changes to your person and or lifestyle may be permanent.
> Dr Gordon Freeman, Black Mesa Research Facility

Figure 4.1 Invitation from an avatar

Journey into avatar land

The workshop began with a relaxed discussion about the types of characters in videogames, and which characters the boys enjoyed the most. These students had well-developed understandings of characterisation and immediately related the discussion to their drama learning, naming the characters according to types: superhero, sidekick, nemesis and protagonist. One of the boys talked about a game that he had seen advertised, where the evil character was actually an army of colour-wipers – he described how the colourful town had its colour wiped away. Another talked excitedly about the Nintendo Wii his family had bought for Christmas. The boys discussed the mechanics of how the Wii worked and what it felt like to play the various games.

The boys were asked to 'think of one story that you like, one character that you like.' The students immediately began animatedly talking amongst themselves and within seconds they had settled on the *Super Mario Bros.* stories, launching into a discussion of which version of Mario and which characters they preferred – Donkey Kong, Mario, Luigi, the nemesis Bowser, and, of course, Princess Peach.

Super Mario Bros.

We were surprised at how quickly the boys jumped on the idea of *Super Mario*, now 25 years old. The boys talked about *Donkey Kong* first (the arcade game in which Mario first appeared as *Jumpman*) but then shifted to the characters from *Super Mario Bros.* We suspect that this was because of Princess Peach!

In the drama room costume box was a piece of peachy chiffon and the boys made a run for it – the chiffon and the Princess Peach character became central to their work, and there was a squabble about who was to wear the chiffon! The boys were also interested that there was a new version of *Mario* for the Nintendo Wii consoles, where Mario and co. appeared as three-dimensional characters. We found it interesting that we both remember the earlier arcade game of *Mario*, and the ghastly machine muzak and very flat two-dimensional characters. When we compared this to the cinematic three-dimensional versions of *Mario* we watched online, we were not surprised that these virtual gameworlds were so enticing.

Exploring the gameworld

By tapping into these students' prior experiences of drama, we hoped to unlock their perceptions of gaming, and non-naturalism seemed to be the perfect approach through which to achieve this. The use of open props such as masks, fabric and chairs encouraged the projection of their own ideas, while widening their scope for creative expression. Working within a group would enable them to consult, explore and express their experiences more effectively than on an individual basis.

To begin the exploration of the gameworld, the group was given the task of creating a narrative of their virtual experiences. To do this, Belinda set the task of creating five quick still images, with each one having a particular set of restrictions. The boys were to shape the narrative loosely based on the traditional structure: normality, interruption, journey, climax, resolution. They were provided with miscellaneous costumes, fabric and levels. They cast the production with the alpha-actor securing the coveted role of Princess Peach after a skirmish for the gown. They were allowed 10 minutes' guided preparation time. The boys were instructed to think about the staging carefully, using different levels and thinking about the usage of space. Princess Peach had anti-gravitational powers and was quite assertive while still remaining somewhat true to her damsel-in-distress coquettish archetype. When given another 30 seconds to improve the scenes, the boys quickly made them more dramatic.

While working improvisationally, the boys worked within the constraints of the gameworld. One boy pointed out 'Donkey Kong always jumps up there,' and the actors rearranged themselves accordingly. When working out their final scene someone remarked that 'Mario always wins,' and this framed the choices that they made in resolving the story. They had been given the option of not having to resolve the story perfectly, but were told that there 'should be some element of resolution.' At the end of this sequence, the boys had brought the characters to life, providing a sequence of images reminiscent of video gameplay.

Princess Peach disturbs school assembly; Luigi comes to Christmas lunch

We asked the students to imagine what might happen if the characters stepped out of the virtual world into their lives. Are these real kinds of characters? How would they fare in everyday situations? What might happen if the characters came into the real world?

In a series of two-minute improvisations we watched each character emerge from the screen into real life. Each improvisation was given a different restriction, including a style, such as in slow motion; and a location, such as at assembly. When Princess Peach leapt from the stage in her gossamer gown in the middle of assembly at this all-boys school she caused a riot!

We watched 'Christmas morning' begin the same as every other year, with some of the family opening gifts, and others still at work in the kitchen. The teenage boy receives exactly what he wanted for Christmas – the latest Nintendo Wii – he delightedly sets it up and immediately begins playing *Super Mario Bros.*, becoming spaced out and drawn into the game and the gameworld. He is playing frenetically and he just can't stop playing. Suddenly, something strange happens. He shakes and shakes all over and Luigi squeezes himself out of the screen. He has come out for Christmas lunch! The boy faints with shock. Other family members also faint when they see Luigi. Unperturbed, Luigi goes into the kitchen, eats dinner and then comes back and plays the game himself.

The nightmare within

The question, 'What do your parents think about computer games?' was to be answered with a short stylised improvisation. We shifted the workshop to the stage, to give the next section an air of theatricality and gravity. The boys were given masks, fabric, levels and music (that they were free to choose). They were instructed to create a sequence from their parents' point of view regarding their forays into virtual worlds.

The boys chose to represent their parents as having a nightmare about the playing. On one side the boy was playing a single-person shooter game – that was repetitive and in slow motion – where the same figure kept getting shot again and again in slow motion, and the boy playing the game kept doing it again and again relentlessly in zombie-like fashion. The mother's voice came over the top chanting 'Go to bed now, go to bed now, go to bed now.' There was horror music playing in the background and the lighting was stark and dramatic. The overall effect was creepy and dramatic and the boys enjoyed every moment.

We were struck by the sophistication of this scene and the extent to which these boys so easily and playfully subverted the dominant discourse of teenagers being mindlessly addicted to gaming.

Virtual worlds, real consequences

These boys showed that they had a critical awareness of the games they are consuming, as well as knowledge of the adult moral panic that surrounds their engagement with these virtual worlds. The boys also showed that they have considerable agency, in fact, when it comes to gaming. When they articulately expressed their perceptions of their parents' fears in a nightmarish episode full of horror, paranoia, scandal and trauma, they also performed it with sardonic wit and humour. They subverted that stereotypical positioning of the playing of games, and undermined the hysteria of those adult fears, thereby empowering themselves. Gaming to them is clearly about play, and Drama provided them with an approach through which to express this. The work in the drama world mirrored what we found through our interviews with the boys: they knew what they were doing in the gameworld, and they were aware of the alarmist view. The drama world enabled them to both exploit and subvert their positions and the world's perceptions of adolescent boys.

Entire worlds are created and just as easily destroyed within the Drama classroom, as the subject provides boys with a powerful avenue through which they can communicate and express themselves. The physical and collaborative nature of Drama seems to funnel their natural exuberance into creative expression more readily than the written word, particularly in the middle years. To free boys' creativity in Drama, however, Belinda finds it essential to contain it within the parameters of a tight structure. These are enabling constraints. She has found that teaching boys who have an abundance of energy, a short supply of concentration and a strong desire to move about the space requires the use of restricted activities. In this way, new skills are introduced, repeated, enhanced, and perfected while a narrative gradually takes shape. Working collaboratively in the context of a Drama lesson is a satisfying experience for middle-years boys, who instinctively represent the natural world in the abstract form of non-naturalism. Transforming spaces, objects and characters is as instinctive to adolescent boys as falling off a chair. At this age, creative expression still flows relatively unhindered, before the late-teen atrophy sets in: 'What do you mean I can transform that chair into a pet Doberman? Can't you see it's a chair!'

Games as text, games as action: the model as applied in this chapter

This unit used drama to playfully explore several issues about digital games. With respect to **games as action**, the assigned task of 'exploring the game-world' demonstrates how through drama a topic like *action* can be explored, together with the importance of situation. Belinda and Jo note how the dramatic performances of the pupils still 'worked within the constraints of

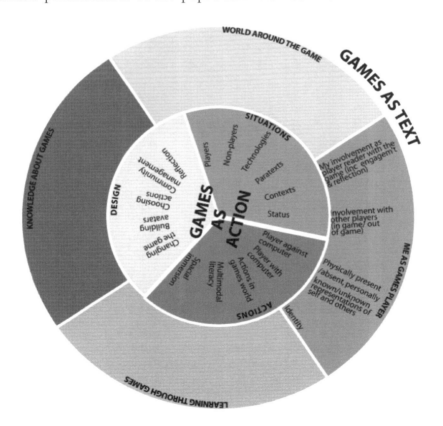

Figure 4.2 Games as text, games as action: invitation from an avatar

the gameworld.' The students' discussion of the importance of constraints, and their acknowledgement of their effects of these constraints, illustrates their awareness of the centrality of *situation* and *action* in gameplay. These concepts are central to understanding how digital game characters (particularly the players' avatars) behave in the game, and how the gameworld (the space of the game) is constructed and used/interacted with (e.g., 'Donkey Kong always jumps up there'). Furthermore, the complex understanding of the game space that is demonstrated by the parodies of how it 'translates' into 'real' space also suggest that the students have an understanding of how digital games are highly *design*ed environments. In relation to the **games as text** layer, the unit shows them working with a focus on *me as games player* and *the world around the game*, as they reproduce and playfully critique dominant perceptions of playing digital games.

Chapter 5

'Gamer hands': Console games as texts and activities that use gaming as a stimulus

Mark Cuddon

Overview of chapter

The challenge in developing a gaming unit of study was to focus on activities and tasks that Year 9 students could identify with, relate to, immerse themselves in and then reflect on in the playing of console games. I wanted them to articulate their thoughts and opinions on gaming, in written and verbal form, in an extensive, perceptive manner. The challenge was also to formalise, incorporate, dignify and justify gaming as a relevant and meaningful 'text' worthwhile of study. This chapter will look at how to introduce gaming as a text into a classroom using the games *The Simpsons: Hit & Run* and *Grand Theft Auto*. A particular focus will be on deconstruction activities (i.e., analysing key aspects of the visual composition of games); and the representations of violence in computer games compared to the incidence of violence in reality.

The gamer observing the game

The following discussion attempts to give credence to the idea that console games and computer games are indeed worthwhile 'texts' to use in the classroom. While some teachers and schools may reel in horror, it is less alarming to discover that traditional pedagogical techniques can be applied to this new form of entertainment and leisure pursuit and that such use of these 'texts' is not at the expense of traditional literacy and analysis.

The unit on console gaming centred around developing a range of activities that dealt with the player as observer, attempting to deconstruct visual and textual content within the games. A goal was to tap into the interests of students through the games they played and also get them to be observers of gameplay, looking at how players use a console and engage and interact with the game.

The challenge for the teacher, who is somewhat divorced from the world of computer and console games and whose sole experience of digital gaming rests with the digital display of a late 1970s KISS pinball machine, was a little daunting, to say the least. The beauty of the task, though, was that it was a way to gear learning directly to student interests. Many of the early discussions centred around games the students were playing and had played in the past. From this general discussion I formulated a brief questionnaire that attempted to tap into where the students were at in their gameplay and where they had come from (Figure 5.1).

I was particularly conscious of the negative publicity gameplay receives in the general media, with many analysts adopting an adverse interpretation on gaming and of players, deemed potentially violent. My secondary aims were to allay the fears and debunk such myths, as 26 Year 9 boys – despite their penchant for first-person shooter games – were in fact discerning and could deliberate on the distinctions between exaggerated fictional violence and the often confronting real-life violence seen in society and excessively reported by the media.

To begin the unit, I designed a survey as an entry into the students' game-playing world. It was an attempt to get them to reflect on this world and allowed me to try to formulate a series of activities surrounding their interests (see Figure 5.1). It was noted in many of the brief questionnaires that the boys in Year 9 were heavily involved in first-person shooter games, car chase/race games and, early in their playing, TV-character-driven games such as *The Simpsons* and *Super Mario*. The discussion that emanated from the boys' gameplay and their questionnaire responses centred on the notion of competition and achievement: for these boys it was possibly an extension of their sporting and educational prowess; to achieve and master a certain game or skill. In order to do this to an extremely high level, however, the boys tended to devote a significant amount of their time to playing and competing to win. Whether this gameplay is at the expense of, or indeed enhances, learning is an area I tried to examine further.

Name the console player(s) you have at home	*PlayStation 2*
Name the portable player(s) you have.	*First edition game boy*
Do you play online games also? If so what?	*Luminary*
What games do you spend most time playing? Why?	*Sport games such as FIFA 08 because it helps strategic skills and managing money*
How do you spend your leisure time? Outline and divide up your evening and weekend leisure time. Include in this as *hours of gameplay* and then *PC download activities*.	*In leisure time I play a maximum of 4 hours. PC downloading – 2 hours. The rest of the day I play in the backyard.*
How old were you when you first used a console game?	*6 years old*
What was the first console game you played? Why did you like it?	*Metal slug at a friend's house*
What skills did you gain in playing your game?	*Managing money, stocks Strategy, hand eye coordination awareness*
Have console games helped you with your abilities as a student? Explain.	*Yes, they have helped in hand and eye coordination (sport) and persisting with studies*
How would you teach a 6 or 7 year old to play *Simpsons: Hit & Run*?	*Teach him where the console buttons are, show him/her the characters in the game and how to play it using the cars. (Jack)*

Figure 5.1 Student response to the initial questionnaire

The interesting aspect of the boys' gameplay was that it was almost never solitary. The boys in their discussion and written pieces constantly made mention of the multiplayer aspects of gaming and the online nature of playing where they interact and communicate and compete against class mates and also players from all around the world. Thus their gaming world, their culture of gamer immersion, was an area that fascinated me; specifically their ability to be part of this technological virtual world, and also their ability to discuss their achievements the next day face-to-face with their competitors/classmates. I was interested to find the Bond University Interactive Gaming Association study on the social nature of gaming, which saw it as a shared interactive pursuit.

The activities

Activity 1: I devised an observational empathy exercise where the boys tried to detach themselves and look at the process of playing the game: attempting to achieve success, mastering a skill, competing against the game, immersing themselves in the world of the game and being allowed by the game to do this. In the case of *The Simpsons: Hit & Run*, students made the connections between the codes and conventions of the TV show, which in turn allowed them to observe and understand how the seven-year-old is immediately familiar with the world of the game.

Activity 2: With the aid of reviews and discussion of the game, the boys were able to make sophisticated textual connections between game and show and they understood the steps the young player was trying to achieve. Thus, rather than players, they were becoming deconstructionalists.

Activity 3: was a follow-up questionnaire, designed to establish the type of console and types of games students preferred. I also had in mind to try and establish a link between action, film and the genesis of gaming. In their surveys on favourite games, many students nominated *Grand Theft Auto*.

Activity 4: Writing a game review of the *Simpsons: Hit & Run* allowed students to reflect on how a game is discussed and what is considered important to the player. Students discussed graphics, animation of characters, sound, adaptation from the sitcom storyline, clothing and the use of humour in their reviews. To aid this activity, I devised a series of questions surrounding the gaming world of *The Simpsons: Hit & Run* and the connections to the TV show itself (Figure 5.2).

'Gamer hands': Console games as texts and activities

- What is 'successful playing' in the Simpsons game?
- What are the common features in the game and the series? Think about setting, dialogue, sound and characters.
- How does the game promote/perpetuate/raise the profile of the series?
- Is the game violent? Examples?
- How is the Simpsons' world recreated in the game?
- How does the cover promote/advertise/profile/entice the potential buyer?
- How do all the elements create meaning?
- What type of humour is in the game? How is it similar to the series? Give specific examples of dialogue and character.
- How does a young player recognise the ways into the game in order to play it? How do symbols create meaning?
- How might you develop a character or enhance a particular aspect of the game?

Figure 5.2 Questions designed to help the students write their reviews

Activity 5: This was an observational exercise where the Year 9 students observed footage of a seven-year-old playing the game. The boys were asked about how the young player interacted with and played the game and about their own experience of playing a console game for the first time. Figure 5.3 outlines the discussion questions the students used for the activity.

The students responded with comments regarding the young boy's desire to stand rather than sit as a way of getting 'closer' to the game and the requirements of fulfilling the tasks in the game. To the students this was seen as pertinent as they noted that the subject was playing the game on a PS2 on a small analogue TV. Therefore, in order to get closer, he utilised the space within the room in a particular way, moving right when his vehicle was required to navigate a right-hand turn. The students also observed the subject engaging in self-dialogue, talking to himself in attempting to overcome a challenge in the game or offering a running commentary of the game. More often than not the subject, in the presence of someone else, constantly talked, offering up points about what he was doing in the game and how he was going to meet a challenge. The students felt that the subject's experience of the PS2 was not inhibited or lacking, as for him the challenge was the game and he hadn't been exposed to the potentials of gameplay in any other way (for example, a PS3 on a 42-inch plasma).

Digital games: Literacy in action

> - How is the young boy's experience of gameplay like yours? What is different? Explain.
> - How is the alternative scenario/gameworld consistent with *The Simpsons* on TV?
> - How are your senses employed when using the game?
> - Why does the handset vibrate?
> - Could you play the game on a small screen?
> - How is the young boy engaged? What is he doing? You might choose to comment on his reaction to symbols, concentration, persistence and choices.

Figure 5.3 Discussion starters for Activity 5

Activity 6: This was a reflective piece of writing on gaming. As mentioned before, the students noted that gameplay is not done in isolation. It can be seen as an interactive, technology-driven social experience which appears, on the basis of student discussion to be highly meaningful, tend to occur within the social realm of multiplayer and online gaming. The students were instructed on the basics of an informative style of writing almost like a review (similar to those found on gamespot.com, The *Age* Green Guide, *The Herald Sun* Entertainment Section and ABC's *Good Game*).

The beauty of whole-class and small-group discussions on gaming is the enthusiasm and excitement it engenders in the class. In turn, students are willing to document, write and reflect on their experiences in an individual writing folio piece based on a 'text' in which they had an interest and an experience they were willing to share. The students were given a wide scope in terms of the genre or style of writing, choosing from a report/expository/instructional guide. All were offered a platform from which to build a piece on gaming (Figure 5.4).

> '*The Simpsons: Hit & Run* borrows heavily from the *Grand Theft Auto* series and, in so doing, brings the world of the Simpsons to life with proper justice.' *gamespot.com*

Figure 5.4 Prompt for student written response from gamespot.com

> 'Even if a game is not multiplayer supported, there are various other features such as downloading new content like levels and guns, posting your scores online to compare with the rest of the world, or just chatting to your friends whilst playing using the Xbox voice headset.
> However, most people use the service for multiplayer gaming, pitting their skills against others around the world and the most successful games on both Xbox consoles or Xbox live, is the *Halo* series. *Halo 3* the latest in the series, is a sci-fi first-person shooter set in the future, and offers great single player gameplay but its multiplayer capabilities has been shown to be its strongpoint.'
> James

Figure 5.5 Excerpt from a student written response

'Gamer hands': Console games as texts and activities

> 'As the game follows the same structure as the GTA entries, much of Hit & Run involves a linear series of missions, with a number of exploration elements to boot. The game uses a basic level structure, with seven total levels, each with seven primary missions. Each level in the game is assigned to one specific character. There's one for Lisa, Marge, and Apu, while Bart and Homer get two apiece. Missions are assigned by interactions with the city's various characters. They generally involve collecting and delivering items to other people or locations, racing other characters, and even getting into full-on car combat situations. In actuality, practically every mission in the game is a direct clone of one of the GTA driving missions. However, the lack of originality in the game's mission structuring is more than made up for by the decisively original style of Simpsons humour. The end result is actually very fun.'
>
> Ewan

Figure 5.6 Excerpt from a student written response – *The Simpsons: Hit & Run*

> 'Call of duty 4 modern warfare has won many awards such as best online gameplay every made. I play this on Xbox 360 and I play with Daniel, Mikey and many other people all over the world. We play by joining each other's match at a certain screen, from there we join a match and we get pared to other players anywhere in the world depending on our rank and score (how good we are). The difference in being good is how well you know all the maps which helps you know where people go so you can be ready and also what I call a happy trigger finger which means that you have a really fast reaction from seeing someone and pressing the trigger. The ranking system goes by score and you get a score by killing people and going certain things in special match types, such as planting a bomb in search and destroy which is 1 bomb and you areas in which to plant it, one team tries to plant it and the other one tries to stop them from doing that. The most annoying thing about online game is Americans because if we join an Americans game we lag which means in simple terms we can't get a kill, doesn't matter how good the player is, this happens because Americans have a much better internet set up. The way people communicate over Xbox is microphones which fit over your head and you talk and listen to what people say through the device.'
>
> John

Figure 5.7 Excerpt from a student written response – *Call of Duty 4*

John's review (Figure 5.7) uses features of the review format and highlights the social, interactive element of the gaming process.

The Year 9 students also commented on the demands of the game on a seven-year-old, believing it to be demanding for an early user of console games. The students were amused and understood the subject's desire to drop back a level in the game because it was 'easier' and 'fun,' and the gameplay was seen to be enjoyable and rewarding if the young respondent could meet a challenge and overcome obstacles in the game.

Digital games: Literacy in action

A fruitful discussion could focus on the social and gaming norms (rules of behaviour) associated with this: a worthy topic for further examination.

Games as text, games as action: the model as applied in this chapter

Mark's project explores the world – particularly the social world – around digital gaming. In relation to **games as action**, two of the activities utilise the notion of *situation* extensively through the examination of the complex spatial and social dimensions of digital gaming. In activity five, watching a short film clip of a much younger boy playing on a small console, the students examined the space where the game is played and the physical responses of the player – both deliberate (by standing close to the screen), and apparently unconscious (moving right when the avatar moved right). Through this students were challenged to reflect on their own processes and practices of digital gameplay. Furthermore, activity six focuses on the importance of the social aspects of play that are highlighted by the *situation* dimension of the model. The excerpts of student writing demonstrate students' awareness

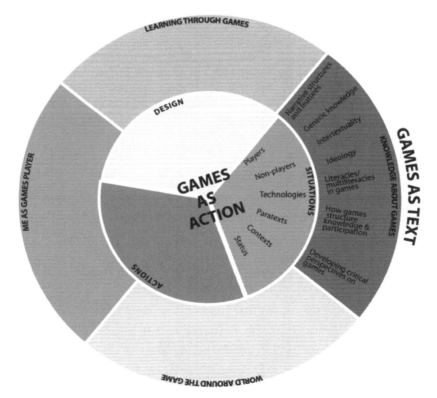

Figure 5.8 Games as text, games as action: Console games as text and activities

of the importance and complexity of the role of situation and its effects on gameplay. Mark sets out to integrate the study of games into the curriculum, in ways that show that such use of these texts is not at the expense of traditional literacy and analysis. With its attention to critical discrimination and deconstruction, its activation of what students already know about generic conventions and representation, and its interest in positioning, intertextuality, reading and ideology, much of the work in the **games as text** area is located within the *knowledge about games* quadrant. The unit also brings up questions in relation to *me as games player* and *the world around the game.*

Chapter 6

Literacy, identity and online fantasy sports games[1]

Amanda Gutierrez and Catherine Beavis

Overview of chapter

In this chapter we focus on the work of Joel, located at an all-boys Catholic High School. We describe his research and classroom projects focusing on online fantasy sports games-based digital texts and culture, and some of the questions these raise about digital culture, literacy and curriculum. Joel capitalised on his Year 11 students' avid engagement with the AFL (Australian Football League) game *SuperCoach* to explore convergences between different media forms, the ways in which players drew on data from multiple sources and their own judgements to play the game, and the ways in which their 'real world' relationships were shaped and mediated by their demonstrated expertise and the authority they drew from their proficiency with the game.

Joel teaches English and Media Studies. He selected his Year 11 Media Studies class for this unit of work, which was completed during the second term of the school year. As the school is an all-boys school, the class comprised of male students in the age range of 16–17. Joel's unit of work revolved around investigating notions of convergence (Jenkins, 2006), which included asking the students to play *SuperCoach* and to discuss the links between other media sources and the ways these merged to influence their decisions in the game. Joel began the unit by looking at elements of control over students' access to and use of media products, and followed this by watching an episode of *Summer Heights High* (Lilley, 2007). From here he discussed with the students their thoughts about new media and how this media is influencing adolescents'

---

[1] A longer version of this account appears as 'Experts on the field': redefining literacy boundaries. In Donna Alvermann (Ed.). (2010) *Adolescents' online literacies: Connecting classrooms, digital media, and popular culture* (pp. 145–162). New York: Peter Lang.

lives. This led into discussion about online communities, with the analysis of several *YouTube* clips.

As Joel described it, elements of the school had something of a 'blokey' character. To tap into the interests of these boys, he chose to look more closely at online communities and convergence through the AFL *SuperCoach* game. He asked the students to reflect on the kinds of skills they were forming through the use of this game and the ways they participated in the online game and the various media sources that were converging to create a particular online AFL game community. Joel was also interested in how the identity constructed online is not necessarily linked to or indicative of the students' physical body, in that the students may not participate in sport themselves but rather use *SuperCoach* as a viable replacement of the physical sporting experience. The *SuperCoach* unit acted as a way to launch an investigation into notions of identity and virtual worlds. Students produced short written pieces and extended analysis pieces as they reflected on these elements.

Online fantasy sports games are part of a multimillion-dollar industry in countries such as the United Kingdom and the United States with games covering sports from basketball through to fishing. While fantasy sport is not as huge a phenomenon in Australia, there are several versions of AFL fantasy online games. *The Herald Sun TAC SuperCoach* Fantasy AFL game, like most fantasy sport games, is a game in which the players attempt to take the role of a coach. The website suggests that '*Herald Sun TAC SuperCoach* is easy to play but difficult to master' (http://supercoach.heraldsun.com.au/). The ease of play can be seen in the fact that the controls are relatively simple. All that is physically required of the player is to create and name a football squad of 33, with 22 on the field, from a list of football players currently on an AFL team in the year of playing. The aim is to create the ultimate team and become the *SuperCoach*. The only real confine is that the team created has a salary cap and the cost of each player varies depending on his statistics from previous real-world games/seasons. The suggestion that the game is difficult to master is due to the convergence with the real world of the game, and the need to be not only AFL literate, but also well-read across all media sources surrounding the game. The end of the virtual season concurs with the end of the real-life season, with the overall winning coach winning not only cash prizes but also his friends' acknowledgement of his status as *SuperCoach*.

This game is a decision-making game and does not attempt to create a world in which students can perform actions with simulated players (or

Digital games: Literacy in action

avatars). Instead, as the screen shot below illustrates, the physical design of the game is relatively basic. It is a game that focuses purely on the management side of AFL; the challenge being to become the overall *SuperCoach*. The actions performed by the 'real' player include the selection of AFL players and their positions on the field and keeping within the salary cap limit set by the program. The students in Joel's class took their gameplay very seriously and became highly competitive. As one student, Jason, said, *SuperCoach* 'is not a game …[it's] a competition more than a game. Not fun. It's serious.'

The students in Joel's class were immersed not only in the virtual game, but in all aspects of the game. They positioned themselves in relation to their 'coaching' abilities which related to their knowledge of the 'virtual' world of the game, but also the 'real' world of the game. Students were involved in processes of creation and consumption of what Consalvo (2007) terms 'gaming capital' – an adaptation of Bourdieu's (1984) notion of cultural capital – which has provided a generative framework within the project for conceptualising important aspects of gameplay (see e.g., Walsh & Apperley, 2008). As Consalvo describes it, gaming capital provides:

a key way to understand how individuals interact with games, information about games and the games industry, and other games players. The term is useful because it suggests a currency that is by necessity dynamic – changing over time and across types of players or games … knowledge, experience and

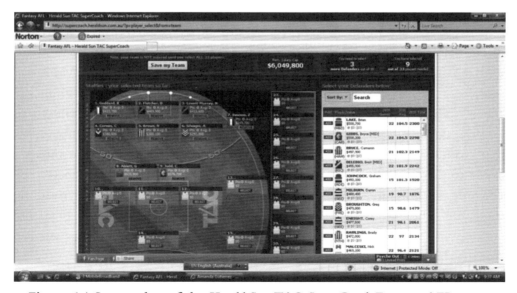

Figure 6.1 Screen shot of the *Herald Sun* TAC *SuperCoach* Fantasy AFL game

> *positioning help shape gaming capital for a particular player and in turn that player helps shape the future of the [games] industry ... Players themselves further shape gaming capital, especially as new media forms offer individuals more opportunities to share and the games world grows even larger. (Consalvo, 2007, p. 4)*

As Consalvo argues, 'Games aren't designed, marketed, or played in a cultural vacuum' (2007, p. 4), which is clearly apparent when discussing with students their immersion in the *SuperCoach* game and the world around it. The virtual 'game,' for the students interviewed in this study, influenced their relationships with peers, their family, other students in the school, and their teachers as they played with and against these other 'coaches' in their daily lives. The students not only had teams in the larger 'Victorian' league, but had also set up a competition just for the school, and a competition against their teachers. So in essence these students had multiple teams for each 'field' of their lives. This allowed them to create their own 'football identity' for each social group with which they associated themselves.

Taking on the role of coach allowed students to take up positions of expertise and authority in relation both to football and their peers. The role of a 'professional' coach, rather than just supporter, provided them with the chance to experiment with the 'expert' knowledge needed in that profession, and the status that affords. For some it afforded them an authority over those who would usually control the power, particularly their teachers and older 'known' participants such as parents, as they advanced higher in the game, and demonstrated more control over the gaming capital than these traditional authoritative groups. It meant distancing themselves from allegiances to particular teams, and instead attempting to take the position of a follower and objective judge of individual 'players' rather than 'teams.'

Two students, Jason and Kevin, mastered the language of this field of knowledge and were so integrated in the *SuperCoach* world during the months of the AFL season that their social group regarded them as game experts. Whenever Kevin stepped into the social identity of the role of 'coach,' he drew on the linguistic devices and language that would commonly be seen in interviews with coaches before and after the games. He did this regularly during the classes. For Kevin, the virtual game and the real game were his passion, even though, as one of the other students commented, he did not 'play the game' in real life. But he did not need to 'play the game' in real life to be an expert on the 'field'; and even with the real game and other professional sports, a professional coach does not need to have been a 'legend' on the physical field, but instead needs to be an expert on how to best play the game, know the players and position them to win games. This game gives those who may not be able to master the real game the chance to become experts in a way that gives them a sense of achievement and a deep connection to the real game.

The reason Kevin was seen as the expert, the person to whom the other students and teachers went for advice, was due to his control over the converging paratexts (Genette, 1997; Consalvo, 2007) surrounding the virtual and real game. The term 'paratexts,' in this context, refers to '… communication and artefacts relating to [a game, that] spring up like mushrooms' around it (Consalvo, 2007 p. 8). Playing *SuperCoach* relies heavily on the intertextual traversing of such texts. To become an expert of the AFL *SuperCoach* game the students needed to not only know how to access the various paratexts surrounding the game, but also critically judge the paratexts. As one student said when asked about making choices about reliable sources from the paratexts available:

> *[I go with] whoever I think has the more valid … whoever I valued their opinion more. I suppose certain people, like Sam Newman, he tends to know not that much compared to someone like who's an actual expert, like a columnist or something. Their background, like their background of the game, most experienced within the game I'll probably value more. (Kevin)*

Students need to have skills that extend beyond traditional 'basic' literacy skills required to simply decode textual material from sources such as *The Herald Sun* and *The Footy Show*. They also need to be critically literate to make judgements about the purpose of each paratext, and any underlying biases the 'expert' commentators may have and the possible reasons. They need to be able to synthesise material from a vast array of sources and genres, ask questions of the texts and make their own judgements about the opinions they receive. The more developed their skills are in relation to this, the better their chances of success.

The paratexts surrounding this game extend beyond regular media sources surrounding the real game. *SuperCoach* has become so popular that there are now columns specifically written for the game in *The Herald Sun* by experts such as Kevin Sheedy, the well regarded ex-Coach of Essendon, radio shows dedicating time to discussing the statistics of the players, and websites. On top of this the students create their own paratexts as they contribute to other online activities such as blogs and forums. The more engaged and involved the players become with the consumption of and contribution to the paratexts, the closer they come to being able to fully engage and be regarded by others as an 'expert' coach in the game. This allows them to feel a sense of achievement at succeeding in mastering the role of coach.

For students such as Jason and Kevin, games function as sites for exploration and 'serious play' – the establishment of authority, status and relationships amongst their peers and in the world of the game. The playing of *SuperCoach* provides a compelling instance of convergence of online and offline worlds; media convergence; and the need for students to be adept in reading, and bringing together and analysing information presented in a variety of forms, from a variety of sources. Playing the game has material effects on students' sense of self; the ways they manage information, knowledge and authority; their relationships in the real world; and the seamless integration of technology into their everyday lives.

Luke, Freebody, and Land (2000) describe contemporary literacies as 'the flexible and sustained mastery of a repertoire of practices with the texts of traditional and new communications technologies via spoken language, print and multimedia' (p 9). The literacy required to play *SuperCoach* entails more than simply decoding textual material from sources such as *The Herald Sun* and *The Footy Show*. Playing the game develops a set of literacy practices that include the capacity to read across media, read information presented in different forms (print, visual, statistics, aural etc.), evaluate material that is or may be heavily invested in other issues (e.g., *The Footy Show*, reportage of individual players, the parade of media commentary and 'expertise'), interpret and translate this information into play, and constantly modify and reappraise in the light of new information. It requires sustained attention to multiple factors over an extended period of time, and is a compelling example of both situated literacy practice with real-world consequences and of the fluidity of gameplay, literacies and identity across online and offline worlds.

Games as text, games as action: the model as applied in this chapter

This unit is strongly anchored in the *situations* dimension of the **games as action** layer. Context, paratexts and status figure strongly in the activities and focus of the work described. As gameplayers, students move back and forth

Digital games: Literacy in action

between the contexts of the 'real world' game as it is played each week; the contexts of the *SuperCoach* competition, including other teams in the world at large, and the competition at the school; and a third, more general context of membership in participatory culture and the digital world. To play the game, they make use of a range of paratexts, with success at the game contributing to their status both in the games world and amongst their peers in the online and physical communities. In relation to **games as texts**, the same activities might be seen as located in the *world around the game* quadrant particularly, as they negotiate and interpret the situated contexts for gameplay, and critically analyse print and multimodal texts, including paratexts, as they engage in a range of literacy practices around gameplay. Success at the game contributes to the development of gaming capital, and participation in the global context of gameplay.

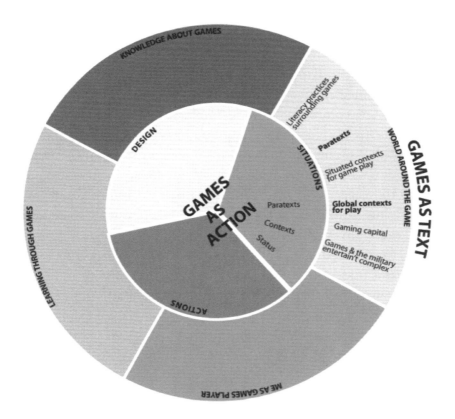

Figure 6.2 Games as text, games as action: Literacy, identity and online fantasy sports games

Chapter 7

A blank slate: Using *GameMaker* to create computer games

Joanne O'Mara and John Richards

Overview of chapter
This chapter outlines a project-based learning curriculum where Year 8 students design, create and use their own computer games. The students, at a regional Catholic, all-boys school, use a free program called *GameMaker* to do this. The games that the boys have been making are engaging to play and some have well-developed themes running through them. In this chapter, the project-based learning approach is outlined, with the discussion focusing on why we make games, approaches to teaching students how to make their own computer games and what students learn from games production. John is the teacher of the program, and Joanne is a Chief Investigator from the project, *Literacy Learning in the 21st Century: Learning from Computer Games*, who has worked with him, researching his practice and the boys' understandings of their game making.

Engaging and sustaining engagement with Year 8
The school in which the project was based specifically caters for the wide range of students who go there – a diverse range of boys who will head out to both the trades and the professions. Being a regional school, the students who attend live both in the city and the surrounding rural areas, and the school families come from a wide range of economic and social backgrounds. Even though there is very little ethnic diversity compared to what is found in Australian capital cities such as Sydney and Melbourne, the socioeconomic diversity in regional schools tends to be much broader than that found in their city counterparts.

It is nothing new to say that engaging boys in the educational process can be difficult. In the junior school the subjects with which the boys usually engage deeply are the practical and physical subjects, however the school has had very good success in building the students' relationship to Multimedia as a subject, and over half of them elect to continue with Multimedia. Whether they are aspiring to learn a trade or a profession, the boys recognise the importance of these skills for their future working lives. Through this project they develop and use a range of skills in multimedia production, requiring practical skills of using the computer tools in addition to creative thinking and making aesthetic choices in the production of their game.

GameMaker with Year 8

For the past four years, every student in Year 8 has created his own computer game in Multimedia class using *GameMaker* software. All of these games have been playable, usable and enjoyable for others – from high-end multilevel games, to simple maze games or click-the-mouse games. This is a project that caters for the variety of learning styles and the wide range of ability found in the school. The many Year 8 boys interviewed throughout this project were all enthusiastic about making their own computer games. They are proud that they can produce their own game. They find the project of making their own computer game to be very exciting and can identify the learning from this work. The boys enjoy making a game that they can use and can share with others.

GameMaker Software

Each year, the school uses the latest version of the *GameMaker* software (the current version is *GameMaker 8*). There is an Information Technology department that supports the teaching staff, uploading the software and setting up the computers. The Multimedia course emphasises to the students that there is a great deal that they can do with what they already have on their computers or what is freely available. This emphasis encourages the students to think about working with what they have and extending their abilities to use the full extent of their computer's capacity, rather than thinking that they always need to buy something new. The potential of 'out of the box' computers is rarely explored to their full advantage by most people, so this approach of encouraging the students to utilise everything that they already have is an unusual one, but one that teaches them to be more resourceful and to learn the limitations of the software.

The *GameMaker* software is designed so that users can easily develop quite sophisticated games with graphics without having to use complex programming languages. It can be freely accessed at http://www.yoyogames.com/make. Because the software is designed to be so user-friendly, the students can focus on designing and making their game rather than the operational aspect of learning to use the program. The free version is very extensive, coming with all of the tools needed to make full games, including quite sophisticated 3D games. There is also a paid version of the game (*GameMaker Pro*), with additional features costing $25. Some of the students buy the full version of *GameMaker* to access the additional features, but they are encouraged to work the free version to the limits before doing this, as most often they already have access to the tools that they need.

An important additional aspect of *GameMaker* is the online community of users and help materials. The students can access excellent online help and *YouTube* videos, leave questions for others and post their games to the site for additional feedback. The ability to connect with this community of users provides additional learning for the students, as they learn how to utilise these additional sources of information and become a part of the *GameMaker* community. The extent to which individual students do this within the frame of their classroom learning is very varied. Some students become very involved in receiving and leaving public feedback and testing other people's games, whereas others may only access help videos.

'Blank slate' software and educational possibilities

GameMaker is what John calls 'blank slate' software — software which is a blank slate full of possibilities, where what you create is totally up to you as the designer and creator. The students used a range of blank-slate software in the Multimedia classes, including *Kahootz* and *Movie Maker*. The openness, and hence versatility, of this kind of software makes it easy to cater for the learning needs of every student in the class. If you download *GameMaker* yourself and tinker with it for a while, you will see the range of possibility. It can be quickly picked up, so, for instance, last year Jo easily had a group of English teachers making the beginnings of their games in a very short PD session. Despite its ease of operation, there is scope within this software to make incredibly sophisticated and aesthetically beautiful games. The students do not have to spend long learning how to make the games, so their time is well utilised in game design. Over the past four years, John's students have made the full gamut of games, from very simple to very sophisticated – the blank slate can be filled in a variety of ways.

Openness and constraints

John has put in place a set of structures and ways of working that create a classroom culture where different students can shine and work together. Every time she has visited John's classroom, Jo has been struck by the collaboration between the students, the level of their co-operation with John and each other and the ways in which they support each other through the process.

Early on in his work with making games, John found that the boys needed some constraints to help them to shape their work, as some students did not know where to begin, given the openness of the software. Like many activities in the creative arts where there are a multitude of aesthetic possibilities, the restrictions provide the scope of possibilities. The task is to produce a game with at least five levels that has interesting sprites (little figures that can move around in the game world) and backgrounds. Some of the boys produce these five levels, whereas others go on to produce games with as many as 30 levels, as such a breadth and range of products are possible.

The boys learn how to plan their game, preparing a flow-chart of how the game moves and how the levels progress. It is important for the production of the game to know how the game will start and end, as each element of the game works towards this. The students also consider the design elements of their game and the aesthetic composition of both the game movements (i.e., its progression through the various game levels); and the overall aesthetics (look and feel) of the game: the use of colour, movement, sound and graphic style at various stages. Most boys have strong narratives woven through their games, and many of the games are very engaging to play. One game made by a student has been further developed by other boys and is in circulation among the group. Boys described this game as being as good as a commercial game and many of the boys Jo interviewed had copies of this game, which they played. Other boys interviewed incorporated ideas and elements that they enjoyed from other games into their designs.

John also conducts a formal investigation with the students about the elements of what makes a game interesting to play and he discusses social issues around gaming with the students. He encourages them to incorporate their gaming into their life in a way that keeps their life in balance, and he encourages students to self-monitor their gaming habits against the notion of whether their life is in balance. The boys also have some formal lessons on the basics of making the games, playing games made by past students, learning specifically how to operate the program and to do things such as moving objects in the game, and having the object interact with other aspects of the game.

'Gone are the days when the teacher is the expert': working in the 'wall-less classroom'

There are two ideas with which we have been working in our thinking around how and why the *GameMaker* project is successful. The first is the idea of the teacher no longer being the expert and how, as teachers, we might deal with that. The second is the idea of what Jo calls 'the wall-less classroom.'

The idea of the teacher no longer being the 'sage on the stage' is central to John's practice in setting up the project with the students. While the students are given several direct skilling sessions where they are shown the work of previous students, the basic elements of making a game and how to go about using the software, beyond this they operate in a self-directed way, setting their own problems and finding their own solutions. John demonstrates the specifics needed to get them started and then takes a 'back seat' while the students embark on their own project, setting their own goals and planning out how they are going to achieve these goals.

One of the things that struck Jo about John's classroom is the ways in which John's shift to the 'back seat' requires active attention to where exactly everyone is at, where they think they are going next and who or what might help them to do this. Part of facilitating the students' success is knowing with whom/what to connect them — often it is another student who has already encountered the same problem, or it may be that the online help has the answer. This attention to the details of where everyone is at, what they have achieved so far, and where they need help, keeps the students motivated and on task as well as enabling John to hook up students with each other to solve specific problems or to access sources of help outside the classroom. This way of working is more involved for the teacher than simply providing the students with the answer or showing them how to do it, but it facilitates self-directed learning in the students, increases their sense of accomplishment and nurtures working relationships between the students in the class.

John finds that some boys have a dependence on teachers to solve everything for them, so one of his aims with the project is to develop their independence and problem-solving skills. He does this through being the last port of call for help – sending them to video tutorials and connecting them to other students in the first instance. When the games are well-developed, John organises several sessions where the students give each other feedback. The students swap their game with the student on the left, play the game and then provide feedback to that student. They are given an evaluation frame to help them to provide constructive feedback.

This shift to a more self-directed learning style has resulted in many of the standard classroom barriers being removed, both by the affordances of the technology itself and by the way in which the projects are managed in the classroom. Jo calls this 'the wall-less classroom,' because the students' work is located both within and beyond the classroom walls, the boundaries of the classroom extending infinitely into the online world. The online *GameMaker* community resources become part of the classroom resources: video tutorials; community wiki and discussions; the possibility for students to upload games made for others to use. Students are learning and doing much more than making their game when they engage with the community – they read instructions, post questions, reply to postings, read reviews, play instructional videos, follow diagrams, navigate the site and play their way through games posted as exemplars. Jo sees the openness of this wall-less classroom as significant, as it replicates 21st century ways of working and seeking information without many of the censures and blocks that schools often impose and which prevent students from engaging with the wider world.

Conclusions

This project turns around the general public perception of young people as merely passive consumers of games, as these boys make, enjoy, share and play games they have made themselves. Being able to work in a trade or profession is an important part of the identity for these boys entering adolescence, and much of the value the boys attribute to *GameMaker* is its value in preparing them for work. Both the ways in which the classroom is organised, and the ways in which in the relationships set up between the boys, their project, each other, their teacher and the outside world, are deliberately structured to be purposeful and prepare the boys for a future working life.

Games as text, games as action: the model as applied in this chapter

John's classroom project deftly illustrates how digital games can be used to teach and learn *design*, with focus and activities primarily located within the **games as action** layer of the model. The use of streamlined game design programs such as *GameMaker* that don't require programming skills allows students to 'focus on designing and making their game.' The process of *design* is thus thoroughly caught up in play and replay. Jo and John's description of the project illustrates how important playing games that other students had created was for students' learning of game *design*. This iterative element of the *design* project also allowed students to reflect on the formal aspects of digital games including *actions* and narratives, as they explored and compared what did not work and what worked in particular digital games that had been designed as part of the class project. While games as action was the primary focus, students also needed to call on the **games as text** dimensions to

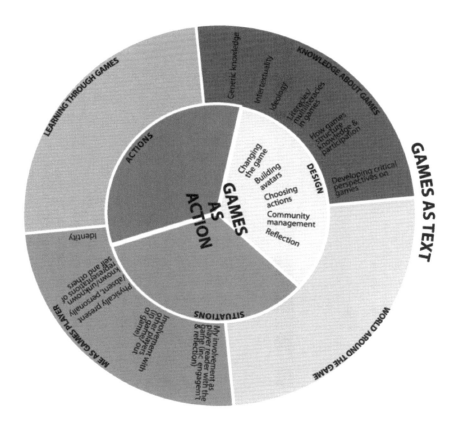

Figure 7.1 Games as text, games as action: Using *GameMaker* to create computer games

Digital games: Literacy in action

activate the knowledge needed to create their games. Implicitly, for games to be effective, students needed to draw on their own *knowledge about games*, and of their own preferences and values in relation to what makes a good game – *me as gameplayer* – in order to design attractive games for themselves and their friends. While many traditional forms of literacy are in evidence, in this unit *design* is paramount, and works across both layers of the model, showing the indissoluble link between the two.

Chapter 8

Game plan: Using computer games in English class to engage the disengaged

Paul Byrne

Overview of chapter

At the end of 2006, The Victorian Association for the Teaching of English (VATE) was looking for secondary schools to become involved in a research program with Deakin University where we could examine the use of computer games in the English classroom. The aim of this research was to improve literacy outcomes for our secondary students in English. I thought this would be the perfect fit for my English Skills class, where students were withdrawn from the mainstream groups. These English Skills students were also disengaged from the learning of English. If we could somehow mesh their interests in computer games with their classroom learning, they might improve their outcomes in this subject. Deakin University ran professional learning days in the computer games lab at the Australian Centre for the Moving Image (ACMI), where we were introduced to the development and theory behind computer gaming. I was a novice to these games but as I played more of them, I began to see the potential that they held for teachers and students. Over a two-year period, as the unit progressed in the classroom, teaching methods were refined to deepen the learning experience for the students. I discovered through this refinement that students were much more engaged in English when examining how computer games worked and their own interest in them.

Background to the project

In 2008, I was teaching a new Year 7 group of 10 students: seven boys and three girls. After assessing the entire Year 7 cohort, the students who ended up in my class were the students who struggled the most in English. As the year progressed their disconnection from English was obvious and no matter how hard I tried to engage them in English games and films, nothing really made them enthusiastic about the subject. Getting them to write anything down was a real challenge. So I really had nothing to lose in trying to engage them. It was time to bite the bullet, and as there were so many boys in my group, it was time to capitalise on their interest in computer games.

Following a workshop on Peter Freebody and Alan Luke's 'four resources model' (Figure 8.1), I began to see how I could connect the use of computer games in the classroom with Freebody and Luke's theories (Freebody & Luke, 1990). Briefly, the 'four resources model' 'provides a principled, learning-centred approach for planning and teaching literacy that encompasses a broad understanding of literacy and moves beyond a single-method approach' (Morgan, Mobi & Jobling, 2008, p. 54).

These categories describe a student's effective participation in a text:

- **Code breaker:** the person must know the relationship between spoken and written language and can interpret graphic symbols and their contexts of use
- **Text participant:** the person must know the meaning patterns operating in written texts
- **Text user:** the person must know and use social and cultural functions of reading and writing practices
- **Text analyst**: the person must know that texts position readers differently, and both constrain and influence them

Figure 8.1 Luke and Freebody's Four resources model
(ref Healy & Honan, 2004)

In *Text Next: New Resources for Literacy Learning* (2004), Annah Healy and Eileen Honan cite Luke and Freebody on the 'four resources model':

> one of the strengths of the 'four resources model' is that it attempts to recognise and incorporate many of the current and well-developed techniques for training students in becoming literate. It shifts the focus from trying to find the right method to whether the range of practices emphasised in one's reading program are indeed covering and integrating a broad repertoire of textual practices that are required in new economies and cultures (Luke & Freebody, 1999, p. 3).

It seemed natural then that I incorporate the 'new culture' of computer gaming as part of 'four resources model' into my teaching practice. It was also extremely fortuitous that at the time there was a huge exhibition at ACMI about the history of computer games called '*Game On*.' I visited the exhibition with Dr Christopher Walsh to work out a 'game plan' so students would get the most out of this exhibition. After this, I organised an excursion where we took the Year 7 and Year 8 English Skills students to the exhibition. It was an extremely successful day and the students were very excited by what they had taken part in.

The activity

Back in the classroom, I was keen to capitalise on the buzz the students were still feeling from their excursion. I told the students I wanted them to give a presentation on a computer game of their choice with conditions. I initially made the proviso that they would have to bring the computer game to school either on a Nintendo DS or PSP or they could play a game that was on the school network. This would enable me to see what game they were going to analyse so I could keep tabs on their progress in class.

However, after a couple of lessons, I had to modify this demand because some of the boys were so passionate about playing their PlayStation games at home they convinced me that it would be okay to present on these games at school. How could I step on their passion? Also some students were keen to analyse web-based strategy games such as *Fantasy Football* and *AFL Dream Team*. By placing these specific conditions on the students, I was constraining their interest in the assignment.

Digital games: Literacy in action

A two-pronged approach

I decided to tackle teaching this program in two ways. For the first prong, I spent a few lessons focusing on how the students were to effectively use a PowerPoint presentation. Most teachers would know that students are fairly adept at using PowerPoint as a piece of software, but stylistically students (and yes, many adults!) still squeeze too many words into one slide, so turning their audiences off. They also do not use this presentation software to its full effect. Students seemed to take on board most of my suggestions to 'uncrowd' their slides. I also used a few examples from *YouTube* to show them how this could be done.

The second prong consisted of the assignment itself. I adapted the 'four resources model' for the students using the following headings and questions that I gave to them in their assignment. The students spent little time in getting to work. The students also worked very well in preparing their presentations and were engaged in what they were doing. They also cooperated well in the groups they had formed.

1. Code Breaking the Game	How do you play the game? What are the rules?
2. Making Meaning of the Game	Have you seen a game like this before? What was it called? What was the other game used for? How did you use it? How was it similar/different to this one? Have you played this game with other people?
3. Using the Game	What is the game's purpose? What is your role in the game when you play it? When do you normally play the game? What is the genre of the game? How do you know this?
4. Analysing the Game	Why do you think the game designers chose to design the game this way? What improvements could you see that would make this game better?

Figure 8.2 Adapting the Four resources model

Gender lines

The students split along gender lines when it came to the subject matter of their games. The boys liked playing games about AFL and Dragon Ball Z and wanted to present on these, whereas the girls were more interested in games like *Imagine Fashion* and *Nintendogs* on DS where they were responsible for raising a puppy from the breed of their choice.

The students' presentations

For the most part the students' presentations went very well. Their PowerPoint slides were fairly uncluttered and there was lots of visual material. Their presentations were also funny and fast moving. Some students, especially the PlayStation boys, had researched their presentations far and wide across the internet. For one boy in particular, who really struggled in English, his presentation was the most writing that he had done all year and it was of a fairly good standard. He had been totally absorbed in the process. Some of the presentations were still too wordy and it was hard to get across to the students that in an oral presentation, visual material in a slide was more important than lots of written material. (Imagine me complaining that these students were writing too much!)

There was one girl who did not like playing computer games although I noticed that when I brought in my *Nintendo* DS to use she became very involved in the game that she was playing. The reluctant gamer, in the end, started quite a good computer presentation, but because of a long absence due to illness it was never completed.

At the end of the year, I had a feedback session with Chris Walsh and Thomas Apperley where I showed them the students' presentations. Their feedback was very positive and was highlighted in an article in the *Australian Journal of Language and Literacy* (Walsh, 2010). They suggested that in the next year I try using PhotoStory for the students to use instead of PowerPoint.

With the next year came a new group of underachieving students. This time I was even more excited to run the computer games unit. The chief difference this time would be that the students would not use PowerPoint to give their presentations; they would present using PhotoStory. I told them that this time they would have to put in spoken narrative with their presentation. This was a lot more for the students (and me) to co-ordinate.

The chief difficulty this time was getting the students to write this narrative. And when it came to them actually recording their narratives we had problems with the computers. The computers could not pick up some of the students' words, as there were faulty sound cards in some of the machines.

However, the results were much the same as the previous year. Students were enthusiastic and involved. Writing for them became less of a chore because it involved writing about something they saw not as work but as play.

Practicalities

Classification of games is an issue. Be aware of the age of your students. For my part, I insisted on games rated G and PG because my students were in Year 7. Insisting on these ratings can also eliminate content with which you may have problems, such as the vast majority of shooter games. If, however, you are concerned about some content of the games that students wish to write about, talk to other teachers to see what they think. It is a good idea to write a letter to parents and/or guardians outlining the unit and the theory behind it.

Not all actualities can be covered, though. I was excited when one of the girls in the class (we shall call her Lucy) who wouldn't say boo to a goose was going to get up and present her game to the group. It was a Nintendo game called *Imagine: Fashion Designer* which is rated G and which looks behind the fashion curtain at the catwalk industry. She was all prepared for her speech. The students were also filming her presentation. As it would happen, in the room at the time was the principal and the deputy principal who were taking a learning walk around school to familiarise themselves with the current literacy program. They were excited at all the hardware in the room, thinking that I must be the most progressive teacher out.

As Lucy prepared to give her talk she handed out the game on a Nintendo console for the whole class to take a look at. Two boys in the class took a particular interest in the game, which gave me no end of pleasure. How terrific, I thought, that boys should be taking such an interest in a game that they usually wouldn't be caught dead looking at. We're crossing real gender lines here, I thought. The two boys then handed me the game that they had been playing, but when I looked down at the screen, to my horror, they had taken most of the clothes off the model. She was standing there wearing very little – just a skimpy see-through bikini leaving little to the imagination. At that particular moment the principal asked me to pass the game down to him. I was seeing spots in front of my eyes, and they weren't on the screen. I had to think quickly. What should I do? As luck would have it I was familiar with the Nintendo, and flicking as hard as I could I put a rather mismatching outfit back on the model. I looked over at the two boys who were grinning mischievously at me. I passed the fully clothed model down to the principal. Crisis averted. The boys could wait till later. Moral of the story: Know the games that you are going to approve. Even the most innocent-looking ones can lay a trap for the unwary teacher.

Assessment of students' work

Assessment of the students' projects was basically descriptive and it was divided neatly into the VELS dimensions Reading, Writing, and Speaking and Listening.

Feedback and the future

For the most part, I found my involvement in this program extremely rewarding. The students became involved in their work at a thinking level that I have not seen for a while, which was especially edifying given the reluctance of the students to produce anything written at all.

'By your pupils you'll be taught,' is also a great maxim here. I learnt as much about computer games and gaming from my students as they did about grammar, spelling and syntax from me. Computer games are not going away. In fact they are taking up bigger chunks of our students' out-of-school time. It is imperative that we give students the skills to step back and look critically at these sophisticated texts in schools and the learning that accompanies them.

I'm glad at least that I took the risk and jumped in to introduce gaming into the classroom. I'll definitely continue this program in future English classes and it will be interesting to see how mainstream English classes work with this unit.

Games as text, games as action: the model as applied in this chapter

The project described in this chapter both builds on traditional literacies and successfully draws on both *action* and *design*. The two stages of first researching a game and then designing and delivering a presentation provided Paul's students with the opportunity to critically reflect on the *actions* that took place in the digital game that they chose. This critical reflection and evaluation of the game developed skills and understandings in both layers identified in both layers of the model – around *action* and *design* in the **games as action** layer, around *knowledge about games* and *learning through games* from the **games as text** layer. By providing them with questions that he had developed using Luke and Freebody's (1990) 'four resources model', including questions both on how to play the game and how to use the console, Paul encouraged students to examine gameplay in a critical manner. The second stage of the project also encouraged the students to explore and develop their multimodal design skills through the PowerPoint presentation that integrated writing with visual design. The students in Paul's classes built on their knowledge

Digital games: Literacy in action

and control of both traditional and 'new' literacies through these activities, extending understandings in these areas and developing a stronger appreciation and understanding of games as a cultural form.

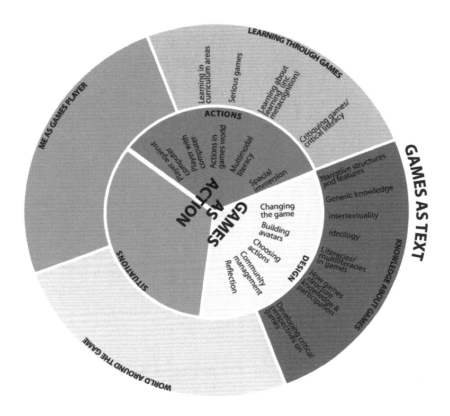

Figure 8.3 Games as text, games as action: Using videogames to engage the disengaged

Chapter 9

Reading in the digital age

Frank Ferretti

Overview of chapter

This chapter will outline the procedures used and the responses, discussions and activities of a group of Year 9 students in a unit of work 'reading,' playing and investigating the video game ecology. The class was a formal Media Studies class offered as an elective. As well as the considerations of investigating production issues of the videogame, a fundamental aim was to explore the students' understandings of narrative and characterisation.

The secondary school curriculum over the last decade or more has had to accommodate the digital age. As all institutions have had to adjust and modify their previously rigidly defined practices, education institutions have had to examine this cultural phenomenon. The conventions and strategies that served teachers so well in the past, particularly in the teaching of literacy, have undergone extensive re-examination and modification.

The impact of the 'information superhighway,' multimedia technologies, Web 2 tools and multimodal visual products, such as videogames, video file sharing and social networking sites have developed their own particular syntagmatic and paradigmatic set of conventions. How students relate to each other, what they value as important and what they see as vital skills to master bear little relationship to the dominant and traditional set of skills that were deemed important decades ago. There is simply more to 'read' in an almost infinite variety of genres than before.

One needs only look at the various educational study designs to acknowledge the dynamic changes that have occurred in teaching practices. Senior

English, Literature and English Language study designs in Victoria all include discrete attempts to 'read' visual texts, predominately film narrative texts. Generic conventions covering visual stylistic elements such as lighting strategies, visual composition and framing, iconography, camera movements and placements have evolved to create specific message-signifying practices. Teaching strategies, particularly within the English classroom, have developed to include a methodology that accommodates this progression.

It is common for literature students to discuss, with a great degree of legitimacy, a visual interpretation (i.e., narrative film) of a classic novel. Narrative elements, characterisation, story and discourse are as fundamental to the experience of playing videogames as watching (reading) a narrative film. The modes of representations have changed but they utilise acknowledged and identifiable patterns, forms, styles and structures as a basis of a consistent syntactic framework, which governs the construction of the work and the 'readings' by an audience.

Methodology

In keeping with the focus of the Media Studies classroom, it was decided in the preparation stage to design a forum from which the students would work. Dr Christopher Walsh designed a forum where the students could register and complete their assignments online (Figure 9.1). The forum has the capabilities to embed digital assignments, video clips and sound files as well as written responses. It covers discussions with games designers, via *YouTube* clips, posts of various games and assignments covering topics such as characterisation in computer games, multiplayer online games and Serious Games. Serious Games relate to games that directly address one or more social value aspects, such as games that highlight natural disasters or issues facing developing countries.[1]

A key element in working in such a way is that it allows students the ability to view responses from other class members and to comment on individual student posts. Students can work on their assignments from home and as the teacher logs in as an administrator, he or she is notified via email of any student additions. The administrator can also ban, modify and respond directly to individual students or a group.

---

1 An extended outline of a related unit of work developed by Christopher S. Walsh is presented in Chapter 11.

Reading in the digital age

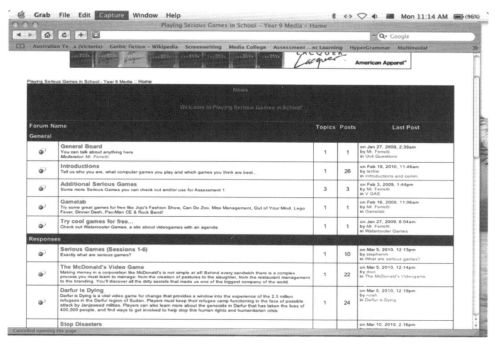

Figure 9.1 The welcome page of the Media students' forum

The level of interactivity in such a format allows the student a variety of avenues to examine their understanding of storytelling elements. David Bordwell, in *Narration in the Fiction Film* (1988), examines the manner in which information is delivered to audiences through films which have an identifiable set of conventions. His analysis is applicable in this area of visual art, as well. He refers to narration as a procedure that incorporates the process of selecting, arranging and rendering story material in order to achieve a specific time-bound effect on the audience. The audience (reader) is able to apply a set of schemata, which Bordwell (1998) defines as 'an organised cluster of knowledge, that has been derived from prior experience and can be directed towards the construction of a story from the information presented' (Bordwell, 1988, p. 31).

Non-linear narratives and creative partnerships

This is vital in the area of computer games as the reader/player is able to navigate in a non-linear way according to their moods, dispositions and interests. The reader applies their understandings of iconography, visual codes and narrative structures. The computer and computer games and the audience in this instance are creative partners. To effectively negotiate all the narrative possibilities inherent in the games the reader/player must employ their understandings of many visual codes.

As the students negotiate their way through the assignments, they are asked to comment on ways that the games use these codes to construct meaning. The methods games producers use are varied; they can be seen as analogous to the techniques employed in the construction of other fiction visual texts. Ultimately they are a means to an end. Whether they are developed within first-person shooter games or real-time strategy games, the reader/player is part of a creative process. Indeed, a striking feature of digital technologies is the ability of the audience to manipulate the narrative of the work by their understanding of the conventions and codes used.

James Paul Gee, in *What Video Games Have to Teach Us About Literacy* (2003), refers to Semiotic Domains, which he defines as

> *a set of practices that recruits one or more modalities (e.g. oral or written language, images, equations, symbols, sounds, gestures, artefacts etc.) to communicate distinctive types of meanings. (p. 18)*

Students invest the texts that they are playing with an acknowledgement and understanding of how image and text production create narrative possibilities. Players are free to negotiate the various levels or stages of a game according to their desires.

The assignments

In this particular class of students aged 14 to 15, students played games such as *The Sims 3*, *Brothers in Arms*, *Halo 3* and, among the serious games, *Darfur is Dying*. (*Darfur is Dying* is a viral videogame for change that provides a window into the experience of the 2.5 million refugees in the Darfur region of Sudan. Players must keep their refugee camp functioning in the face of possible attack by Janjaweed militias. Players can also learn more about the genocide in Darfur that has taken the lives of 400,000 people, and find ways to get involved to help stop this human rights and humanitarian crisis.)

One of the assignments was entitled 'Characterisation in Computer Games.' Students were given a choice to play their favourite games and a series of questions was asked (Figure 9.2). The students would post their responses online and the teacher could comment on each response. All students could see the responses and teacher comments.

Reading in the digital age

> *Drawing on one of the games you play regularly, answer the following questions:*
>
> What elements combine to create the character in your game? What do you focus on?
>
> How much control do you have over your characters' (a) appearance (b) actions (c) values, personality and attitudes and (d) life choices/chances?
>
> In what ways can you exercise this control?
>
> What assumptions does the game make about your relationship, as a player, to different characters? How do you find out about this?
>
> Do different levels and settings have an effect on the characters, or on your response to characters as you go through the game?

Figure 9.2 Assignment questions from 'Characterisations on Computer Games', designed to stimulate online discussion

Students found the ability to control actions and appearances important. This is likely tied to the narrative of the game. In the game *Halo 3*, a particular player was interested in the fact that all the characters have distinct personalities. Two of the characters are 'friends.' The player noted that you 'crack jokes' and you 'look after each other.' The relationship between the characters changed according to the levels played and the decisions the player made. Games of this type offer a variety of narratives each time they are played.

Other games of interest were games that used historical events as a basis for the storytelling. *Brothers in Arms*, a WWII game, develops particular narratives with individual characters. Another student describes a back-story to the game. There is an assumption that the historical details are important in establishing the personality of the character. Notions of 'career soldier' and nationalism are not far from the surface of such a game.

> *You grew up in America and your father was a soldier in World War 1 and now you're a soldier in World War 2. You are in a military operation that went horribly wrong and you and your squad fight through Holland to stay alive ... some assumptions you make as your character are that you are a veteran who fought in D-Day and you wouldn't make another soldier do what you wouldn't do ...*
>
> *Your character is in a burning town with houses burning, in others you're in a dark city and it's pouring with rain and the music puts you in a mood that sometimes is slow and sad and you feel like giving up and then some is more energetic and you feel you can accomplish the mission.*
>
> *Kim*

Figure 9.3 Extracts from student postings on the forum

The narrative threads referred to by the student in the first extract relate to real events that may lead to other learning disciplines and can be the start of extension activities within the class. The students also became aware of production elements, which further aided them in constructing different levels of meaning. Elements such as music and lighting within the game were of significance, as the student's comment in the second extract demonstrates.

It is evident from the experiences of the students that digital technologies such as computer games have the capacity to change the way we negotiate non-linear narratives and in turn express ourselves. This approach incorporates notions of construction, genre, audience and stylistic elements which not only invite more detailed and interesting interpretations, but also include diverse disciplines within the framework of the analysis.

Conclusion

The teacher sensitive to the development of multimodal texts is in a position to let the technology itself take on far more importance as an educational tool. In areas such as computer games (as well as web authoring and using Web 2 tools, among others) the production conventions can become a central focus of learning and analysis, on equal footing with literacy skills. This type of teaching can employ different emphases, where one stream of inquiry can look at the literary construction of narratives while another might consider the sociological impact of the media used, whether they are feature films, news broadcasts, or internet programs, such as blogs and wikis. This form of humanities/social science inquiry is in itself a valuable mode of learning. The other area of interest concerns the actual production methods of the media products. This technical application has traditionally been the province of the Media/Visual Arts teacher. In recent years, it has become (or should have become) the domain of all teachers, with the proliferation of the new technologies and the requirements of industry, and tertiary educational institutions, wanting students to be competent in all forms of traditional literary and visual literacy skills.

Tana Wollen (1994), in her article *Interactivity and the New Media*, distinguishes between 'linear narratives' (or 'regressive modals, 'as they are dubbed – unfairly and rather crudely – by the producers of the new technologies; because one sits and laps it up) and the new 'progressive modals' where everything from image, sound and colour can be controlled, allowing for greater interactivity between the product and the audience/user. She cautions us on the nature of this engagement, stating that interaction, like any dialogue, can range from the banal to the provocative: Narratives are

Reading in the digital age

universal, but some narratives are better than others. The contemporary teacher has this phenomenon to contend with. The resultant changes in the dynamics of what is taught, how it is taught and why it is taught have become major considerations in the classroom. If a school curriculum values innovations, all forms of narrative multimodal texts need to be accommodated.

Games as text, games as action: the model as applied in this chapter

Frank's curriculum unit revolves around students playing and reflecting on serious games. The ways it acts upon its view of **games as action** and **games as text** is evident, for example, in the assignment on 'Characterisation in Computer Games' which asks students to critically reflect on various formal elements of characters in digital games (e.g., 'How much control do you have over your characters' (a) appearance (b) actions (c) values, personality and attitudes and (d) life choices/chances? In what ways can you exercise this control?'). The assignment requires students to play and critically examine

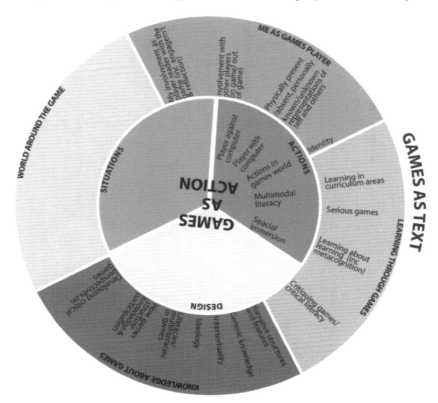

Figure 9.4 Games as text, games as action: Reading in the digital age

particular serious games that have been assigned. This type of assignment allows students to examine and reflect upon *action* in digital games, and superbly illustrates how serious games may be used to ask questions about the medium of digital games as well as the world. In doing so, in relation to **games as text**, the unit directly addresses *learning through games*, while also calling on *knowledge about games*, and *me as a games player*. It links literacy and production through students' playing, reflection and multimodal commentary on play.

Chapter 10

Game-O-Rama!

Maureen Cann

Overview of chapter

Game-O-Rama situates gaming in the educational setting by focusing on student engagement and learning. It draws on the principles of constructivism, cognitivism and connectivism and foregrounds the way in which literacy practices are inextricably linked to social and cultural contexts and complexities. *Game-O-Rama* positions computer games within the domain of multiliteracies, and illuminates ways English teachers can craft their contexts to engage students in multimodal meaning-making and knowledge and skill transfer. It also has a particular focus on the 'learning to learn' attitude and the literacy practices in which young Australians engage.

This chapter provides a vignette of virtual learning delivery to a class of Year 7 boys who range in developmental levels. The learning was centred around *Game-O-Rama*, a joint student- and teacher-designed and maintained wiki. *Game-O-Rama* is not about playing computer games in school. It is about interacting with them as a resource that can teach students about their learning and their world through virtual worlds. It moves the philosophical frameworks of learning into the digital age by weaving together principles distilled from constructivism and cognitivism with principles of connectivism. I refer to this as the 3Cs (Figure 10.1). The affordances of computer games enable *Game-O-Rama* to craft an instructional environment with a social learning network where students collaboratively engage in, explore, explain, extend and evaluate new knowledge and learnings in a virtual environment.

> - *Constructivism* is a philosophy about learning that proposes learners need to build their own understanding of new ideas. (http://iisme.5ecommunity.org/index.php?area_id=569)
>
> - *Cognitive theorists* view learning as involving the acquisition or reorganisation of the cognitive structures through which humans process and store information. (Good & Brophy, 1990, p. 187)
>
> - *Connectivism* presents a model of learning that acknowledges the tectonic shifts in society where learning is no longer an internal, individualistic activity. How people work and function is altered when new tools are utilised … Cognitivism provides insight into learning skills and tasks needed for learners to flourish in a digital era. (Siemens, 2004, p. 5)

Figure 10.1 The 3Cs

In *Game-O-Rama*, the students' expertise and personal knowledge and the teacher's cognitive knowledge and instruction are collectively and collaboratively distributed. The students bring to the classroom their lifeworld knowledge. The teachers bring cognitive knowledge from the subject English and their instructional knowledge. This coupling brings a special uniqueness to *Game-O-Rama*. Darling-Hammond (2000, pp. 166–173) refers to educators as 'people who learn from teaching' rather than as 'people who have finished learning how to teach.' Hattie extends this notion, claiming that 'the more the student becomes the teacher and the more the teacher becomes the learner, then the more successful are the outcomes' (Hattie, 2009, p. 25). Hattie's evidence of quality learning dovetails with George Siemens' learning theory for the digital age – connectivism. Siemens talks about learning

> *as a process that occurs within nebulous environments of shifting core elements – not entirely under the control of the individual. Learning (defined as actionable knowledge) can reside outside of ourselves (within an organisation or a database). (Siemens, 2004, p. 3).*

Game-O-Rama aligns with a number of the principles of connectivism:

- Learning and knowledge rests in diversity of opinions.
- Learning may reside in non-human appliances.
- Learning and making connections is needed to facilitate continual learning.

- Ability to see connections between fields, ideas, and concepts is a core skill.
- Currency (accurate, up-to-date knowledge) is the intent of all Connectivist learning activities.
- Decision-making is itself a learning process. Choosing what to learn and the meaning of incoming information is seen through the lens of a shifting reality. While it may be the right answer now, it may be wrong tomorrow due to alterations in the information climate affecting the decision (Siemens, 2004, p. 4).

The *Game-O-Rama* wiki provided what Siemens refers to as the 'learning ecology' within which the boys can be active. As well-connected young Australians, the boys transferred their personal knowledge into a social network; they collaboratively managed and filtered knowledge and utilised the 'flow of knowledge' by connecting their peers with the right knowledge for their context in order to create a computer game.

Game-O-Rama also sits within the cognitivist paradigm, where humans process and store knowledge in multiple ways. The cognitive approach to multimodal learning is based on the premise that meaning is created and transferred through the active process of understanding and interpreting sets of signs and signals. This is called semiology. Linguistics is one branch of this science. Swiss linguist, a founder not only of linguistics but also of what is now referred to as semiotics, made the connection between linguistic capital and what Siemens calls the flow of knowledge: 'The laws which semiology will discover will be laws applicable in linguistics, and linguistics will thus be assigned to a clearly defined place in the field of human knowledge' (;).

More recent theorists, concerned about how literacy pedagogy might address the challenges brought about by technology and increasing cultural and social diversity include The New London Group. In 'A Pedagogy of Multiliteracies' (New London Group, 1996; Cope & Kalantzis, suggested five semiotic codes that work together in a multimodal text to construct meaning: linguistic, visual, audio, gestural and spatial. Cope and Kalantzis' contributions also cut across systemic levels, providing a descriptive framework for viewing the broader contexts in which national and international education systems now operate. For example, the Australian Curriculum: English aims to ensure that students:

> *learn to listen to, read, view, speak, write, create and reflect on increasingly complex and sophisticated spoken, written and multimodal texts across a growing range of contexts with accuracy, fluency and purpose. (Australian Curriculum Assessment and Reporting Authority [ACARA], 2010, p. 1)*

It defines texts as:

> *written, spoken or multimodal, and in print or digital/online forms. Multimodal texts combine language with other means of communication such as visual images, soundtrack or spoken word, as in film or computer presentation media. (ACARA, 2010, p. 6)*

'Create' is described as 'develop and/or produce spoken, written or multimodal texts in print or digital forms' (ACARA, 2010).

In *Game-O-Rama*, the boys belonged to a virtual community that provided them with a conduit to conduct both routine in-school and out-of-school activities. The *Game-O-Rama* wiki acknowledged that the role of digital technologies (ACARA, 2009).' The boys contributed meaningfully to their community of learning by collaborating, making their own decisions, generating questions, discussing what they learned, considering the effects of their knowledge, applying their knowledge to other situations, and sharing and storing knowledge for both leisure and future learning. *Game-O-Rama* represents a clear recognition that learning is a socially situated, actionable and active process and one linked to building learning, identity, agency and new teaching pedagogies.

In *Game-O-Rama*, different processes and learning styles are inextricably linked with the principles distilled from constructivism, cognitivism, connectivism and curriculum to provide a foundation for digital multimodal authoring.

Game-O-Rama was structured so that students could explore, explain, extend and evaluate their progress. This provided the learning ecology within which different processes and learning styles were interwoven with the three interrelated strands of Learning Language, Literature and Literacy. These strands later came to form the core of the Australian Curriculum: English.[1]

---

1 The Australian Curriculum: English Foundation to Year 10 is organised into three interrelated strands that support students' growing understanding and use of Standard Australian English (English). Together the three strands focus on developing students'

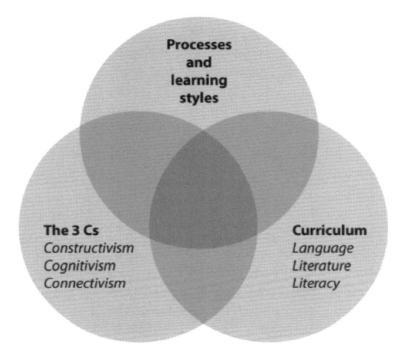

Figure 10.2 Integrating the 3Cs

They also resonate with the tenets of constructivism, cognitivism and connectivism. Three statements from the American National Research Council (NRC) report *How People Learn* (NRC, 1999) summarise this synthesis:

1. Students come to the classroom with preconceptions about how the world works.
2. Developing competence in an area of inquiry requires: a) a foundation of factual knowledge, b) understanding facts and ideas in the context of a contextual framework, and c) organising knowledge for retrieval and application.
3. Helping students learn to take control of their own learning by defining goals and monitoring their goals and monitoring their progress in achieving them.

---

knowledge, understanding and skills in listening, reading, viewing, speaking and writing. The three strands are: 1) Language: knowing about the English language; 2) Literature: understanding, appreciating, responding to, analysing and creating literature and 3) Literacy: expanding the repertoire of English usage. (ACARA, 2010, p. 2)

The 5Es

The 5Es were originally proposed by the Biological Science Curriculum Study (BSCS) and are in alignment with the general capabilities that underpin flexible and analytical thinking, a capacity to work with others (Ministerial Council on Education, Employment, Training and Youth Affairs (MCEETYA) (2008), p. 13) and the rationale and aims of the Australian Curriculum: English. (ACARA, 2010, p. 1). The 5 Es, and the ways in which they were present within the *Game-O-Rama* unit are outlined in Table 10.1, below.

When assessing student achievement, assessment criteria can be developed from relevant standards and associated tasks. For the purpose of this project, learning experiences within the 5E model were purposely designed into a framework, and in this chapter they are mapped against the Australian Curriculum: English–Year 7 achievement standards for listening and speaking, reading and writing. This provides a basis for giving clear instruction and feedback to students about:

- Text immersion/text creation (students speak about, write, create and reflect on texts).
- The draft Australian Curriculum: English provides a scope and sequence for students' work to be evaluated by the same criteria regardless of the medium.

Game-O-Rama could be used to assess against the achievement standards for listening and speaking, reading and writing at Year 7 within the Australian Curriculum: English. At the same time, the *Game-O-Rama* unit demonstrates how the Australian Curriculum: English standards can be seen to align with the 5Es. The table below illustrates how *Game-O-Rama* might be used to:

1. Identify the quality of learning evident in the student's response in relation to relevant parts of the achievement standard for Year 7 in the Australian Curriculum: English, and
2. Incorporate the processes of listening, speaking, reading/viewing and writing/creating – also known as the language modes – into teaching and learning in an integrated and interdependent way.

Table 10.1 The 5Es and how they translate into practice in *Game-O-Rama*

The 5Es	Key Learning in *Game-O-Rama*
ENGAGE in game-based digital literacy to: Promote curiosity. Elicit prior knowledge about the student's literacy identity. Illuminate the understanding of concepts, processes and skills to be learned.	Students compared a computer game with Disher's (1997) *The Apostle Bird* and simulated a particularly difficult situation in the novel within a game concept that played with the existing narrative but introduced multiple choices and possibilities to be enacted through gameplay. Students visited an interactive exhibit on computer games. They identified the distinctive features of computer games; their narrative elements: genre, plot, character development, point of view, and the semiotic systems at play: linguistic, visual, auditory, gestural and spatial. Before going to the exhibit, students brainstormed what they should look for. Responses included: How do multimodal texts work? How do the semiotic systems work together? How do computer games use textual elements to position the readers, viewers or players? How do computer games reflect our social and cultural values?
EXPLORE game-based digital literacy by: Working collaboratively. Using prior knowledge to generate new knowledge. Actively exploring the gaming environment.	Students conducted research into a game or a genre to verify their prior knowledge and understandings about gaming and to explore questions and possibilities. Each student prepared a knowledge base consisting of: the historical background of the game; how the game came to be named; hardware needed to play the game; the game's subject, plot or scenario; and elements of the game's design, including the multiple semiotic systems and questions regarding an author's motivation for creating a game. To facilitate cognitive collaborative learning, consideration was given to knowledge and skill transfer and the building of trust relationships to facilitate this transfer. Class meetings ensured students were committed to a cyber-safe and supportive learning culture.
EXPLAIN new literacy learning and understanding by: Actuating known and new knowledge. Generating new ideas. Exploring possibilities to guide deeper understandings.	Using http://wetpaint.com students reported their research findings on interlinked edit-able wiki pages, which became the sum of their knowledge. Students' approach to creating the wiki entries was shaped by instruction that described and scaffolded the software, including ways to navigate the wiki through hyperlinks, words and phrases, the knowledge base and the structure and language features of each entry. Students discussed their research online and edited information supplied on the *Game-O-Rama* wiki. When editing other students' work, they adhered to class protocols.
EXTEND by applying new literacy learning and understanding to: Conduct additional activities for new knowledge. Add breadth and depth. Refine skills.	Students applied knowledge and understandings gained in *Engage*, *Explore* and *Explain* to create a computer game. *Explore* strategy questions apply here as well, because students used their knowledge base to propose solutions, make decisions and negotiate the focus and scope of their game. PowerPoint, *GameMaker* or Flash was used to create their games. This knowledge was fed into the broader school network via the wiki space.
EVALUATE learning how to learn through: Learning conversations. Reflective practice. Assessment criteria.	Evaluation was ongoing and included assessment of students' new knowledge and skills derived from this process, application of these new concepts and change in students' thinking. Students and teachers collaboratively determined how much learning and understanding had taken place. This informed future learning. Assessment criteria were developed from relevant achievement standards.

Table 10.2 Framework for assessment, informed by the *Australian Curriculum: English*, version 1.0 (ACARA, 2010).

Australian Curriculum: English – Year 7 achievement standard			
Text Immersion (which integrates the phases Engage and Explore)	Modes	Relevant elements of the achievement standard	Evidence of student learning in *Game-O-Rama*
	Listening, Speaking, Reading / Viewing	Students listen to, read and view a range of spoken written and multimodal texts. They: • *Identify and explore representations of events, characters and settings and express their own responses to these representations* • *Interpret and explain key ideas and issues* • *Make inferences, drawing on textual evidence, increasing their awareness of purpose, audience and context, and their knowledge of a growing range of literary techniques* • *Synthesise information, ideas and viewpoints from a variety of texts to draw conclusions* • *Use their increasing vocabulary, and accumulated knowledge of text structures and language features, to support their interpretation and evaluation*	Contributing personal knowledge and life experiences in discussion and verbal exchanges about the distinctive features of traditional and multimodal texts Listening to and identifying main ideas and concepts, expressed by others, respectively recognising different perspectives, asking clarifying questions summarising and building on others' ideas, providing and justifying other opinions. Comprehending, interpreting, acquiring and synthesise information from book literature and websites to actively explore the gaming environment. Critically consuming and actively reflecting on particular games, their histories and intertextuality. Discussing and analysing the social value and the semiotic aspects of multimodal texts using relevant and appropriate metalanguage with a focus on how audience and purpose impact on game composition.
Text Creation (which integrates the phases Explain, Elaborate and Evaluate)	Speaking, Writing / Creating	Students create well-constructed spoken, written and multimodal texts. They: • Interact with others in groups to exchange and substantiate ideas and opinions • *Make oral presentations to share and promote points of view, supporting these presentations with selected evidence* • *Select appropriate vocabulary to show shades of meaning and opinion, to express ideas clearly and to engage and elicit a response from the audience* • *In expressing a point of view, draw appropriately on personal knowledge, textual analysis, and other relevant texts they have experienced* • *Effectively use a variety of clauses and sentence structures, paragraphing and punctuation to sustain meaning and to support the structural coherence of the text*	Applying knowledge of multimodal texts to construct a spoken report on their research findings. *Maintaining a class wiki presenting:* • Authored wiki pages with images, and hyperlinks to websites outside the wiki *Computer games demonstrating:* • New understandings of social, cultural contexts and problem solving • Understanding of game structure complete with storyline, imported and self-designed graphics, sound and textures and subsequent paratexts • Understanding of the interplay semiotic systems • Working knowledge of PowerPoint as a complex and interactive system *Reflecting on the effectiveness of learning:* • As a team through the building of trust relationships to facilitate the transfer of knowledge • For the individual learner through identifying areas for improvement in future learning

Figure 10.3 shows the relationship between the 5Es, the three interrelated strands of Language, Literature and Literacy and the students' knowledge, understanding and skills in listening, reading and viewing, and speaking, writing, creating and reflecting on *Game-O-Rama* as an online multimodal text.

	Text immersion			Text creation		
	Listen	Read	View	Speak	Write	Create
Engage	✓	✓	✓			
Explore	✓	✓	✓			
Explain				✓	✓	✓
Extend				✓	✓	✓
Evaluate	✓			✓	✓	✓

Figure 10.3 Achievement standards for listening and speaking, reading and writing explicit in the 5Es

Game-O-Rama actively immersed and cognitively engaged the boys in their own learning. In their games the boys created sophisticated stories and demonstrated deep-level thinking and strategy skills. They showed a knowledge and mastery of the semiotic elements – linguistic, visual, auditory, gestural, spatial – and how they cohere into textual composition to construct meaning. All of the games drew on diverse programming and technology skills, and the boys' facility with technology was critical to the learning in *Game-O-Rama*.

Your Mission and Wizardry are two examples of games students designed. They are reflective of all the boys' deep engagement with digital literacy practices and illustrative of their proficiency in creating a multimodal text. Both games are third-person survival games that embark on challenging quests and draw inspiration from the boys' literary knowledge of the fantasy Both games balance interaction with a diversity of characters, sound, scripts, messages, plots, settings, spatial layouts and linguistic features. In Your Mission, for example:

Digital games: Literacy in action

wizardry

Once a long time ago. The land was ruled by Wizards who treated all fairly and justly. Then one of the Wizards, a man called Astaroth, seized power from the other wizards in a bloody coup. Only one wizard survived and, to save himself, he used the last of his magic to hide among the people. His name was Seth and this is his story about the defeat of Astaroth

Oh No!!!

You have lost the game! There was an avalanche. You get buried, freeze and reincarnated in 3010 AD. You die from hypothermia somehow ...

Click HERE to try again

GAME OVER

Your Mission

You are to use your mouse to guide yourself across the surface and reach a ring at the end of the area. REMEMBER to beat this game you can't think what I want you to think. You have to think differently. Think of the possibilities. Be a MAD GENIUS!
Click on the circle to continue.

Figure 10.4 Examples of student work from *Game-O-Rama*

> You play as a mad genius.
> As a mad genius you use a mouse to guide yourself across dangerous terrain to reach an empowering ring. After each level you are confronted with a higher challenge such as, an avalanche which could see you buried when meteors appear out of nowhere. To beat this game you have to be imaginative and think differently or be reincarnated in a different time.

The games the boys authored evidenced the utility of 3Cs as a cooperative leaning model in a digital age. The boys collaboratively engaged in, explored, explained, extended and evaluated their new knowledge and learning in a virtual environment. They built on their prior knowledge, transferred their new knowledge and understanding and demonstrated a grasp and control of this new knowledge in the use and creation of a computer game. In *Game-O-Rama*, the boys developed a new way of learning and the knowledge, understanding, skills, behaviours and attributes needed to enable them to reach the intended learning outcomes at a Year 7 level in English and to succeed in life and work in the 21st century. *Game-O-Rama* suggests that 3C-based learning and teaching can have a positive effect on the mastery of curriculum, ICT and personal and social competence, critical and creative thinking, and students' interest in and attitudes towards learning.

In *Game-O-Rama*, students used their literacy identity to engage in and explore ways of listening to, reading and viewing the conventions and structures used in traditional and multimodal texts. They explained and transformed their knowledge about texts into digitally literate practices by creating complex and sophisticated computer games with fluency and purpose. Students' reflection on their learning showed that they clearly perceived the learning ecology created by gaming as active and effective in supporting cognitive collaborative learning.

Within the project, different processes and learning styles were inextricably linked with the theoretical rationale principles distilled from constructivism, cognitivism and connectivism and national curriculum design elements to develop a pedagogy that was appropriate to digital multimodal authoring. As a dynamic project, *Game-O-Rama* recognised the collective cognitive capability present in an English classroom and illustrated how to cultivate computer games as a multimodal text in the English Curriculum.

Games as text, games as action: the model as applied in this chapter

Maureen's *Game-O-Rama* project emphasised digital multimodal authoring. This focus provided for an evenly balanced emphasis on both **games as**

Digital games: Literacy in action

action and **games as text**. The multimodal authoring strongly aligns it with the principle of *design*. The *design* element of the project took place on two levels. First, the *Game-O-Rama* website took the form of an in-class wiki which the students collaborated to populate. This format allowed them to integrate text with multimodal elements like photos, screenshots, and audio-visual clips. Second, the game *design* projects required students to use PowerPoint to design digital games and demonstrate their multimodal literacies. *Design* enables a close alignment with the guidelines and requirements of the Australian Curriculum (English), in relation to multimodal texts and literacies and the ways in which assessment criteria might be met through *Game-O-Rama*. In relation to **games as text** the unit particularly addresses foci in the quadrant, *knowledge about games*: literacies/multiliteracies in games, generic knowledge, narrative structures and features, intertextuality and developing critical perspectives. The emphasis throughout the unit is creativity and production as well as analysis and research.

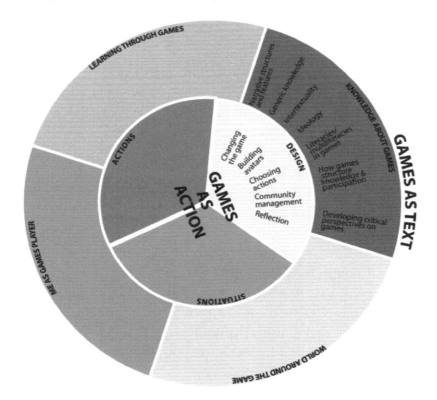

Figure 10.5 **Games as text, games as action:** *Game-O-Rama*

Part 3

Extending work with games

Chapter 11
Including serious games in the classroom

Christopher S. Walsh

Overview of chapter

Although serious games are well established in gaming culture, they are rarely focused on as an object of study in secondary classrooms. This chapter explores ways of researching, playing and working with popular serious games with secondary Media students. It presents three popular serious games and outlines a unit that incorporates serious games in the classroom using online message boards. Importantly, it also outlines how classroom teaching and learning in the serious games unit is closely aligned with the Victorian Essential Learning Standards for the Arts (Media) and Communication. In conclusion, I outline the unit's final assessment tasks, where students were required to either make an argument for including serious games in the classroom, write a proposal for a new serious game or design their own digital game using *GameMaker 7*, a free popular game design software available online.

Introduction

The digital games industry is well established and highly successful at producing immersive, entertaining, educative and compelling digital gaming experiences through serious games. Serious games have the ability to engage students as gameplayers and active participants in their narrative structures. This is because they present two- and three-dimensional virtual environments, appealing characters, relationship to other texts outside the game, music and graphics, and certain social movements. Through serious games, students are actively engaged in gameplay on their own and/or collaboratively where they explore and negotiate risk, possibility, identity and subjectivity in virtual worlds that resonate with the digitally mediated literacy practices of their lifeworlds. Researching, playing and designing digital games places students into new literacy domains that are positioned outside traditional reading, writing and multimodal design practices, because games are enacted through gameplay and actions in virtual and non-virtual worlds (Walsh, 2010).

This chapter supports the notion that playing serious games can make an important contribution to learning (non-entertainment purposes) outside the serious game itself as gameplayers play/interact with the games. This is because serious digital games – through their gaming technology – can be seen to encourage focus, empathy, compassion and imagination in the game-player in ways that supersede more traditional print-based texts, as well as media texts. Approaches to digital games in education often involve the task of analysing or discussing one or two specific digital games in the classroom. My position is that the skills and literacy practices around digital games, particularly serious games, are best understood as overlapping with other forms of digital media and global youth culture.

Playing serious games in school

Within the unit, Year 10 and 11 Media Studies students played three popular serious games: *The McDonald's Game* (Molleindustria, 2006); *Darfur is Dying* (Ruiz, 2006); and *Stop Disasters Wildfires* (Playerthree & United Nations ISDR, 2007). The *McDonald's Game* requires the gameplayer to manage four different aspects of running the McDonald Corporation: agriculture, the slaughter house, the chain store, and the corporate entity (which also includes the PR machine). The idea is that to be successful at playing the game, players will have to engage in practices that are unethical and circumvent environmental and health concerns in the pursuit of profit (or capitalism). In *Darfur is Dying*, gameplay occurs in two separate sections that illustrate the daily struggle for subsistence in a time of genocide in the Darfur region of Sudan. In the first section, the player chooses a Darfuri man, woman, or child who then plays the game by foraging for water. Gameplay consists of running across a barren landscape with a water can searching for a well, while hiding to avoid jeeps carrying Janjaweed militia. If unsuccessful, the player is captured and a screen pops up indicating what will likely happen to the character. The second section of the game takes place in a refugee camp where the gameplayer must maintain the camp's health by obtaining food and water and/or building shelters using the limited resources available. In *Stop Disasters Wildfires*, gameplay is through scenarios where the gameplayer helps towns prepare for and prevent property damage, death and injury during a wildfire. gameplay here is about assessing the disaster risk and trying to limit the damage.

All of the unit's activities and assessment tasks were organised around a message board hosted by ProBoards (www.proboards.com). Working with Frank Ferretti and another media teacher at the school, (see Chapter 9 for discussion of a related unit taught by Frank at a different year level), I decided to use a message board to generate additional interest from students by providing all of the unit's resources (YouTube Digitals, walkthroughs, FAQs, etc.) on various forums. Instead of responding in print, students completed activities online and posted their responses and assessment tasks online. The ProBoards site required each student to register with their school email. Only registered users were able to access the site with a unique password.

Designing the unit

Using backward design (Wiggins & McTighe, 2005), the Serious Games Unit was crafted to provide learning experiences to meet specified purposes or benchmarks outlined in the Victorian state standards while simultaneously aligning teaching and learning with something central to many students' life-worlds – digital games. The unit was organised around one big question and several inquiry questions:

Big question
- Should serious games be included in the school curriculum?

Inquiry questions

- What do students learn from playing digital games (serious and entertainment) that they do not learn from reading print texts?
- How do digital games (serious and entertainment) engage the player/user?
- How do serious games encourage players to think about the events (war, famine, drought, etc.), objects (people, corporations, countries, etc.),

principles and philosophies presented in the games – outside the game?

Upon completion of the unit, students needed to be able to argue the above questions eloquently, drawing on their personal gameplay experiences, games research and the unit's online resources. Within the unit, students also explored the larger ecology of digital games (serious and entertainment) by examining and producing digital texts that extended outside the serious games on their own. This included examining:

- FAQs
- Walkthroughs, cheats, hacks
- Blogging done by designers, players, or institutions
- YouTube digitals
- Publications, promotional trailers
- Objects created for games

What follows is an outline of the unit. This is presented in exactly the same way it was presented to the students. It is presented in this format with the idea that readers may decide to adapt it and use for their own contexts. Please turn to the Resources Section at the back of the book where Appendix A outlines how the unit is aligned with the Victorian Essential Learning Standards for The Arts (Media) and Communication up to and including Level 6.

The unit: playing serious games

Because each of us has a different experience playing digital games, this unit has been designed to allow you to participate at your own speed. The unit is divided into sessions where you will need to complete/respond to all activities by the end of each set of sessions. There are also 2 assessment tasks you are required to submit on the due date. All of your responses/assignments need to be posted on the class message board.

Session 1: Getting started
To participate in the unit please:

1. Register for the class discussion board. Only registered users from your class will be allowed to make postings. Once you have registered for the board, click on the profile icon and modify your profile by clicking on the link. The correct time is GMT+11. Feel free to design and upload an avatar (you might want to use this game to create your avatar http://www.gametimearcade.com/games/3788/south-park-character-creator-3.html). *Please remember that under no circumstances are you to post any personal information on this website. If you are unsure about this, please discuss with your teacher and consult the Secondary School Acceptable Internet Use guide.*
2. Explore the class message board to discover the depth and scope of your participation in the unit.
3. Review the unit activities (by session) and the 2 assignments and their due dates. Prepare any questions you have for the unit and post them in 'Unit Questions' under the category 'General.'

Sessions 2–6: Exploring serious games

During these sessions, you will have the opportunity to investigate and play three different serious games.

The task is to play the different serious games and investigate how the games – through gameplay – engage the player (you) by focusing on required tasks, whether it is a learning task, an exploration of public policy/politics, a virtual tour through a planned environment or a call to take social action. There are a number of small tasks, located on the message board, which you will need to complete as you investigate and play the serious games.

Task 1: Exploring Serious Games

What are serious games?

Read/view the following resources and then answer the following questions: What are serious games? If you were to design your own serious game, what would it be about?

Resources:
- GameZombie.tv presents a conversation with Ben Sawyer http://uk.youtube.com/watch?v=HDFPSg6y-50FATWORLD

- Game Trailer http://uk.youtube.com/watch?v=ZPAzhFZnkYI
- Drunk Passenger on a plane http://uk.youtube.com/watch?v=cEDMVSTY890
- Global Conflicts: Palestine http://uk.youtube.com/watch?v=3ANbDOKmJ6s
- Critical Mass Interactive's Serious Games Demo http://uk.youtube.com/watch?v=imjNXvDrRaM
- Serious Games Institute http://uk.youtube.com/watch?v=B1L_SRT1ve4
- Serious Game from Wikipedia http://en.wikipedia.org/wiki/Serious_game
- Serious Games (July 14th 2008) http://flux.futurelab.org.uk/2008/07/14/serious-games/
- What Are Serious Digital Games? http://uk.youtube.com/watch?v=HbCvKz6UOFQ

Task 2: Play the three games listed and answer the following questions for each game

McDonalds Game (http://www.mcdigitalgame.com/index-eng.html)
Darfur is Dying (http://www.darfurisdying.com/)
Stop Disasters Wildfires (http://www.stopdisastersgame.org/en/)

- How do you play the game? What is the procedure of playing? What actions are/are not possible?
- How does your character interact with the game or what role do you take inside the game?
- Do you learn anything from playing the game? Explain.

Task 3: Considering Serious Games

There are many production elements used in digital games – much like cinema/TV. 'Camera' positioning, lighting effects, soundtracks, visual composition/graphics and point of view all have impact on the player/spectator.

Choose one serious game (*McDonald's Game, Darfur is Dying, Stop*

Disasters Wildfires or a game from the list of 'Additional Serious Games' (see Appendix A in the Resources Section). Produce an assignment/project in one of the forms below, paying particular attention to the following questions:

1. What elements combine to create the character in your game? What do you focus on?
2. How much control do you have over your character's (a) appearance (b) actions (c) values, personality, attitude/s (d) life choices/chances.

In what ways can you exercise this control?

1. How much growth or change is possible for your character, or for characters in the game? How is this signalled in the game? Given character change or growth has been an important feature of the extended narrative, how is this played out in your game?
2. What assumptions does the game make about your relationship, as a player to different characters? How do you find out about this?
3. Do different levels or settings have an effect on the characters, or on your response to characters as you go through the game?

Word Equivalent – 800 – 1000 words
Students can submit their investigations in the following formats

- Written
- Data presentation
- Discussion
- Group/Individual

Sessions 7–10: Exploring digital games (entertainment) and characterisation in the genre

In this section of the unit, you will also be asked to discuss a game of your choice and focus on your character and the ways in which characters are created and act within the entertainment games genre. You will need to think about characterisation in an entertainment digital game you *currently* play outside of school. This may be an online game such as *World of Warcraft* (http://www.worldofwarcraft.com/trial/, *Teen Secondlife* (http://teen.secondlife.com/), *Guildwars* (http://www.guildwars.com/), *Runescape* (http://www.runescape.com/), etc., console games on Wii, PlayStation, X-Box or mobile (handheld games) on the Sony PSP, GP2X, Nintendo DS, etc., or games you play on your mobile phone.

Task 4:

Answer the following questions about one or two of the games you play on a regular basis:

Digital Games you play
- Name one or two digital games you play regularly. Briefly describe where, when, who you play with and for how long.
- What game are you best at? Would you consider yourself to be an expert on any game? Why?
- Are there games you want to play that you can't? Are there consoles that you want that you don't have? Is your Internet connection fast enough? How do you know these better games exist?
- Would you like it if there were more people you could play games with? What games?
- How do you access and play better games than the ones you have access to?

Exploring the larger ecology of digital games
- Do you ever ask people for help to play/finish/level up the game? (tell us which game and why)
- Do people ever ask you for help? (tell us which game and why)
- Where do you find information about finishing/playing/levelling up without asking anyone?
- What is the best source to learn about how to play the game, outside playing the game itself?

- Are you a leech, or do you contribute or add to FAQs or walkthroughs? (Please share any FAQ or walkthroughs you have accessed by providing the link, resource publication, etc. or any you have made yourself.)

Considering the Avatar (thinking about characterisation in digital games)
- What's your favourite Avatar out of all of the games you play? Why do you like it so much?
- What are the cool things he/she/it can do?
- Do all games have Avatars?
- Do you prefer games where you configure your own Avatar over those that provide choices? Why?
- How do you know what Avatars can do?

Characterisation in digital games
- What elements combine to create the character in your game? What do you focus on?
- How much control do you have over your character's (a) appearance (b) actions (c) values, personality, attitude/s (d) life choices/chances?
- In what ways can you exercise this control?
- What assumptions does the game make about your relationship, as a player, with different characters? How do you find out about this?
- Do different levels and settings have an effect on the characters, or on your response to characters as you go through the game?

Sessions 11–12 (Research Project)

Task 5: Research Project – The Digital Games Revolution

Aim: You have discussed and examined serious games and entertainment genres. The aim is for you to produce a research project which incorporates what you have learned. This project can be completed in any of the mentioned forms. It also includes a production component and the possibility of designing a serious digital game.

Consider the following questions in light of the debates about digital games and digital gameplayers. Many groups and individuals have expressed a variety of views about the games revolution and its social and cultural implications. What do YOU think?

For this assignment, you have a choice. You may complete 1, 2 or 3 below. Regardless of choice, you must present your research project. Your presentation should be a multimedia presentation where you design a text that lets us know what you have learned in the unit.

Choice 1 (School Board Presentation): Should serious games and entertainment games be included in the school curriculum?

1. What do students learn from playing digital games (serious and entertainment) that they do not learn from reading print texts?
2. How do digital games (serious and entertainment) engage the player/user?
3. How do serious games encourage players to think about the events (war, famine, drought, etc.), objects (people, corporations, countries, etc.), principles and philosophies presented in the games – outside the game?
4. What makes a good digital game? What does it need to be enjoyable and attractive to play? What are some examples? Refer to Jesper Juul's (2003) classic games definition on the message board by discussing your game according to his 6 games elements:
   a. **Rules**: Games are rule based.
   b. **Variable, quantifiable outcome**: Games have variable, quantifiable outcomes.
   c. **Value assigned to possible outcomes**: That the different potential outcomes of the game are assigned different values, some being positive, some being negative.
   d. **Player effort**: That the player invests effort in order to influence the outcome. (i.e., games are challenging.)
   e. **Player attached to outcome**: That the players are attached to the outcomes of the game in the sense that a winning player will be 'happy' with a positive outcome, and a losing player 'unhappy' with a negative outcome.
   f. **Negotiable consequences:** The same game (set of rules) can be played with or without real-life consequences.

Choice 2 (Proposal for Nintendo): Serious games can teach us something about the world we live in. Think of a serious game not yet developed and write a brief proposal following the outline below.

Narration format – do not write bullet points! Write as if it is a proposal for a digital game that you would give to Nintendo. Be professional in your written words and grammar.

Suggested format:
   a. Title.
   b. 1st Paragraph/slide: The name, theme, and learning goal of your game.
   c. 2nd–4th Paragraphs/slides: The roles – heroes, villains, obstacles (like in *Mario* – the mushrooms are obstacles to Mario's success). Draw/construct/animate the character (paper/pencil, Flash, Adobe, etc.)
   d. 5th Paragraph/slide: Explain how a player gains points throughout the game.
   e. 6th Paragraph/slide: Explain how the unique Nintendo interface (touch screen for DS or the Wii remote) will operate in this game.
   f. 7th Paragraph/slide: Description of the 1st level of the game. This should include a description of the setting, the look of the characters, the tools that the hero uses, what obstacles he/she will encounter, and what they have to do in order to get to the next level.
   g. Themes to Choose From: Anything you think is important or serious!

Choice 3 (Game Design): Design your own Digital Game (entertainment or serious)

Ever thought of designing your own game? It is not as hard as you think! We suggest you use YoYo's programme *GameMaker* 7. It is a free download. YoYo has a number of digital tutorials and you do not need to know any programming languages.
   a. Use *GameMaker*'s tutorial entitled 'Your First Game' from http://www.yoyogames.com/Game Maker/. Follow all of the steps ☺
   b. Present your game to the class

Discussion

The Year 10 and 11 Media Studies students involved in this project reported that they enjoyed the chance to research, play and design digital games in school. In both classes, students actively used the message board to access, respond to and upload their assignments. Even though this unit was completed in a media class, the activities with which the students engaged also developed the literacy skills that students were required to demonstrate to achieve these standards. For example, students identified the ways in which complex messages are effectively conveyed and they applied this knowledge to their communication. In the assessment tasks students also had to consider alternative views, recognise multiple possible interpretations and respond with insight. They used complex verbal and non-verbal cues, subject-specific language, and a wide range of communication forms. Through the assessment tasks' questions, students had to explore, clarify and elaborate complex meaning, demonstrate their understanding of the relationship between form, content and mode of digital games, and select suitable resources and technologies to effectively communicate their findings. Students' posts on the message board used subject-specific language and conventions related to digital games to present and communicate complex information. Students also provided constructive feedback to others and used feedback and reflection in their design and review of each other's digital games made with *GameMaker 7*.

Games as text, games as action: the model as applied in this chapter

Games as Action: This chapter primarily focuses on *situation*, and is strongly anchored in it, although some of the assessment tasks engage with action through a detailed discussion of character, and choice three for the final research project involves *design*. *Situation* is brought to the fore in two ways: first, by advocating and engagement with, and reflection on, paratextual materials as legitimate research materials in the serious games unit; and second, by specifically asking that the context of play be considered in sessions 7–10, by asking questions such as: 'What is the best source to learn about how to play the game, outside playing the game itself?' In doing so, the chapter similarly utilises and develops many elements identified within the **games as text** layer, requiring players to call on their *knowledge about games* in order to operate in the fourth quadrant, *learning through games*. Most strongly in the games as text layer, the unit asks students to become reflexive about *the world around the game*, through their examination of games and gameplay, and of

Digital games: Literacy in action

paratexts such as walkthroughs, cheats and hacks. It harnesses and extends the literacy practices surrounding games to articulate with and strengthen formal requirements for literacy achievements, as outlined in State curriculum requirements – the VELS.

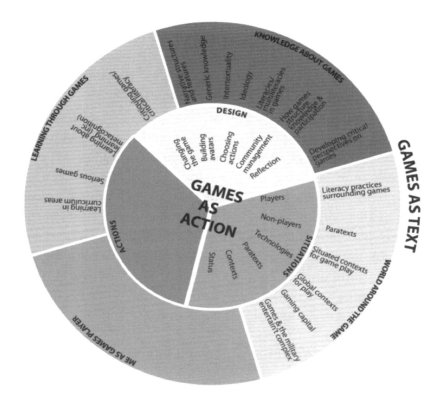

Figure 11.1 Games as text, games as action: Exploring serious games

Part 4

Perspectives from beyond the classroom

Chapter 12

Computer games and the after-school club

Jeanette Hannaford

Overview of chapter

As a teacher working in the primary sector, and with a strong leaning towards critical literacy pedagogies, exploring what children were accessing in their internet play seemed essential to understanding their world and their needs. The research showed that although children highly value and enjoy this play, they do have problems in its management that call for adult support. Ongoing observation of this play is recommended to inform parents and educators about the discourses which children are encountering, and to allow analytical discussions around this content to develop.

Introduction

Over the course of the winter semester I held a computer club on Friday afternoons during which Grade 3 students freely played on their own choice of internet game sites. The computer club proved popular and successful within its context as an after-school activity and I received much positive feedback from both parents and participants in regard to the children's enjoyment of the club. Among the benefits were the opportunities for the children to interact with each other about their internet play experiences, and the implication that their choice to play internet games in their unstructured time was valued and confirmed by the school body, something which appeared reassuring to both children and parents. During the club I observed and noted the children's interactions and self-talk, and interviewed the children about their play.

Imaginative play and identity

My initial questioning addressed whether the children in their own time played make-believe games that were influenced by the narratives of their favourite sites; in the same way that they might after reading an enjoyable book or seeing a favourite film. Justin was the only boy to play (or to admit to playing) imaginative games influenced by his favourite internet play sites. Justin was a big fan of www.linerider.com. This reminded him of 'roller coasters and slap-stick comedy from olden-day cartoons.' Justin made up his own play influenced by this game, such as pretending to accidentally drop a flaming baseball when there were lots of trucks underneath. During one computer club session the children were asked to draw something influenced by the games they liked to play. Justin drew a very free, line-based picture (Figure 12.1) and spun a complex story into it. His description (below) brings to mind Dyson's conclusion from her research into children's involvements in superhero narratives; 'Children's imaginative play is all about freedom from their status as powerless children' (Dyson, 1997, p. 166).

Figure 12.1 Justin's game-inspired drawing

'Well, um, like it's supposed to be a race of line riders but Bionicles are trying to attack the Line Riders. This guy here [top left] at the beginning tried to push this guy off. This one pushed off most recently is about to be attacked by one of the bosses. These are two small Bionicles, that one is bad and that one is good, and this Line Rider is about to be grabbed by the deputy bad boss – the victim is saying 'rats.' This other good guy is maybe going to save the victim but he doesn't know if he should or he shouldn't because he is sort of a robot and a human is an unknown thing for him. He doesn't know if he is a poor little mitty thing or a secret invader and enemy.'

Figure 12.2 Justin's story

Digital games: Literacy in action

Noa drew a new character for www.MyScene.com. After she had described her character a little, she paused and noted as an aside that the character was actually like her (Figure 12.3). When I encouraged Noa to continue telling me about the character, her description moved more and more into the future, describing things like 'she is really clever and gets really good marks in her exams.' It appeared that Noa was fantasising for herself a confident, secure future triggered from within the space of the game narrative.

Figure 12.3 Noa's drawing: 'Actually, she's like me.'

Issues around game content

The one guiding rule of the club was that children were to play only games that their parents would typically permit them to play at home. A few popular sites, particularly www.youtube.com, were forbidden by a small percentage of parents without one-to-one supervision, but games found through common children's portals were not restricted by any of the children's parents. During one-to-one interviews, however, a number of children discussed the problem of having accessed and viewed images in games that had distressed them.

These were not necessarily visuals that they felt obliged to report to their parents, but pictures designed to be shocking within the context of child-directed websites, for example skulls and devil images. One boy, Zane, said that he didn't want to elaborate on it; he was just conscious that such images were 'out there.' He said that the thought of these images made him feel 'bad' and he did not think that 'people should be allowed to put whatever they want on the computer.' His stress over the issue was apparent.

Therefore, an explicit teaching area the club highlighted for me was the need to support children with their management of distressing images. One game that I observed a child playing involved the amputation of an arm that had been pierced with an arrow. It was a game which I, and another teacher who was in the room at the time, found very disturbing, even though it was accessed through a popular children's game portal. On subsequent investigation, I discovered, however, that it carried an initial warning that the game was 'very graphic in nature and viewer discretion is advised.' It may be reasonably deduced that the conceptual language 'graphic' and 'discretion' is beyond the comprehension levels of most eight-year-olds.

As Buckingham (2000) notes, the contemporary notion of childhood is a culturally determined construct which is maintained through the lenses of adults. It is common that discussions around internet play and children are presented as crisis dialogues authored by adults in the popular media, such as the calls for a public debate on childhood and child rearing orchestrated by Palmer and the *British Daily Telegraph* newspaper in 2006 (Fenton, 2006, http://www.suepalmer.co.uk/) which proclaimed the need for children to eat 'real food and have real play (as opposed to sedentary, screen-based entertainment).' It could be argued that these discourses have been constructed by adults for adults, and take a limitative focus of imposing restrictions on children, rather than viewing what else might be done to address problems.

Critical literacy pedagogies that empower children to question the views with which they are presented are one way in which educators may encroach upon value-laded arguments. Carrington (2008), in an article about youth blogging, investigated the first few results of a Google search using the terms 'kids, children and blogs' and found the resulting articles were crisis-laden and did not include the point of view of the children involved. Carrington raises the issue of 'who owns children and their activities' in her account of 11-year-old and 13-year-old bloggers; however, at the eight-to-nine-year-old 'entry-level' age into independent literacy, concerned adults can still claim

Digital games: Literacy in action

responsibility to monitor children's internet play, and use opportunities which may present themselves for opening dialogue into issues of concern.

One site that prompted conversation with other adults, principally to check whether they also found the content surprising and inappropriate, was a game in which the players' aim was to satisfactorily mix alcoholic drinks (Figure 12.4).

Yasmin – If he doesn't like the cocktail he falls down.

Kimberly – Maybe he is drunk.

Yasmin – Or he turns into an angel and flies away.

Lauren (calls out to all the girls) – Gin and Tonic! That's a normal drink.

Kimberly (using a gravelly voice) – Vodka!

Teacher – What is this game teaching you?

Yasmin – How to make drinks. Maybe he might like lemon juice.

Lauren – How did you keep him alive?

Kimberly – I think I put in tonic and then gin.

Lauren – I've never gotten the right mix. He always shakes his eyes to see if anyone is coming. He's a dead man, yes! I don't think he will stay alive on this game because it is alcohol. If you drink too much – perhaps they are trying to make it half reality – so it teaches that alcohol can kill as well as how to mix drinks.

Yasmin – I put all the orange things in.

Lauren – I'm searching for the whisky.

(Yasmin indicates that she has succeeded to which Lauren responds – Red Hot!)

Figure 12.4 Yasmin, Lauren and Kimberley talking about Bartender

Livingstone's review (2003) of the emerging research into children's internet usage cites several projects (Stald, 1998; Stern, 2002; Turkle, 1995) which suggest 'that the internet offers a comparatively safe yet private place for children to experiment with identity' (Livingstone, 2003 p. 151). While confronting to adults, this play with the potentially risky discourses of 'sophisticated drinking' demonstrates that this is clearly an area of interest to these children on the brink of the teenage world. There were marked changes in performance enacted by the girls during the episode. There was a definite air of excitement and they seemed to transform themselves into imitative adult role-play, exemplified by Kimberly's use of a gravelly stage voice to say the word 'vodka,' and Lauren's use of the phrase 'Red Hot' to praise Yasmin's success in the game.

Further issues around identity

Games whose narrative content overtly illustrated gendered ways of being seemed to be more prevalent in games which the girls played than at the sites which were most commonly chosen by the boys in the group. On one afternoon two girls were playing a game found on a popular children's game portal which is sorted into range of game classifications. This game was under the classification Adventure Games, a classification that is then further divided into three sub-categories, one of which is Kissing Games.

> Teacher – Why is she going off with the boss now?
>
> Caitlyn – She probably didn't mean to, she just has to because he's her boss and she doesn't want to get fired. They (young female avatar and similarly aged male character) were kissing so he got fired because he (the boss – a much older character) caught them, so then she (young female avatar) went out with him (the boss).
>
> Teacher – Is it a good thing to make a game about, a good topic?
>
> Caitlyn – Yes, because it is fun.
>
> Lauren – The old man was in love with the girl, the co-worker. If your boss likes you, never kiss in front of him (giggles) with your colleague.
>
> Researcher – Is it normal for people to kiss at work?
>
> Lauren – Probably … or maybe not.
>
> Caitlyn – They probably don't kiss behind people's backs while they are on the phone.
>
> Lauren – If you like someone, you shouldn't kiss while you are working if it's a really important job. You should just kiss when you are out of work, not when you are in the work.

Figure 12.5 Field notes from Caitlyn and Lauren's conversation when playing Kissing at Work

The girls in this example, who come from different school classes and social networks and do not usually play together, were attentive to their interactions during the playing of this game. Much of their conversation involved a critical reading of what was being represented on the screen, which they were filtering through their existing knowledges about what might be suitable identity performance for a young, female employee, and the girls were alternately monitoring their responses to build a shared picture of appropriate behaviour. It may be considered that the girls were engaged with, rather than immersed in, the narrative at this time (Douglas & Hargadon, 2001).

On another occasion, Lauren, having tuned into the boys' conversations and slipped over to see what they were doing when they became rowdy, typed the address of a site that the boys had been discussing into her browser window, but then she stopped, saying to herself 'this isn't for girls.' When I questioned her about this, she said that the site was inappropriate for her but not for the boys. She said that her mother had taught her that the boys could do what they want, but that Lauren must choose appropriate, 'elegant' actions. This anecdote demonstrates an interesting moment of intersection between gameplay and identity in which the child's primary discourse maintains its hold over her actions (Gee, 1996). While I include this example knowing that some readers may focus on the selection of advice given to the daughter, out of loyalty to the participants in my research, I would like to suggest that a perspective which also may be adopted here is of guidance given by the mother according to her own best judgement. In any circumstance, it is included to illuminate the argument of the wide possibilities that dialogue around gameplay might accord.

Reflections

As a teacher currently working with this eight-to-nine-year-old age group, I was enabled by the computer club to observe students at play from a more distanced and observational position than my usual teacher/facilitator role allows. The overwhelming observation I made during the club project was the high significance the practice of internet gameplay had for the students themselves. Beyond being simply a pleasurable pastime, game play seemed to be an activity which the children valued for its potential to help them attain an elevated status in their peer group. This was evident both in the popularity of the club and in the way that children behaved within it, seeking to know what others were doing, and what they were capable of, and the prizing of technical virtuosity. It is beneficial that educators are aware of the agency that children have in this practice, and perhaps reflect more frequently on how we can position ourselves within our students' Discourse of Computer Play, instead of manufacturing situations incorporating such technologies in our own Discourse of Teaching.

Chapter 13

Narrative and computer games

Clare Bradford

Overview of chapter

Narrative is central to the lives of humans, who make sense of experience through the stories they tell. Many computer games, too, rely on narrative: players tell stories about their experience in the game, and genres such as action adventure and role-playing games incorporate narrative elements (including characters, plot, settings) into their design. Like all texts incorporating narrative, the stories woven into game design are informed by ideologies and value systems. Despite the importance of narratives to many computer games, narrative theory alone does not account for how games work or how players experience them, but is best used in conjunction with other theoretical fields.

Humans shape their worlds through narrative: they make sense of their experience by ordering events, by attributing cause and effect to actions and occurrences, and by valuing some elements of narratives (persons, places, events) over others. Narratives are generally produced retrospectively – that is, they begin with an end point, and show what led to this point and how. For instance, we might produce a narrative based on a game of football or tennis or golf, in which we account for how the game ended: who won, by how much. We may not begin our narrative with the result of the game, but it will be shaped by our knowledge of its final moment. Our narrative will incorporate individuals involved in the game (players, possibly coaches and spectators); it will identify turning-points and focus on telling passages of play. It may even make connections with other games in the past, comparing players or their actions. It will often place this game in a broader context: a playing season, the history of a team or sporting club or individual. The narrative of the same game might be told in many different ways, depending on the storyteller's affiliations and vantage-point. The *story* of the game comprises its components: actions, characters and settings. The term 'narrative' refers to *how* stories are unfolded: the choices of language, point of view, sequencing of events and strategies of characterisation which shape meaning.

I have begun with this broad view of narrative and its centrality to human experience because the history of computer games and of critical studies of computer games is bound up with concepts of narrative that go far beyond the analysis of games. Many of the early debates in the field focused on whether computer games were best explained by narratology (narrative theory) or by ludology (theories of games and play) (Simons, 2007; Raessens, 2006). By the time these debates occurred, narratology was already several decades old, with its origins in 1920s Russian formalism, whereas game studies is a new field which developed from the 1980s. From the beginnings of game studies, scholars noted the difficulties that arose when they attempted to map computer games onto models of narrative which took the novel (and, later, the film) as core examples. Over the last decade narratology has developed and expanded as scholars working in disciplines such as psychology, medicine, legal studies and anthropology, among others, have combined narrative theory with other knowledge systems (Heinen & Sommer, 2009). The foundational concepts of narrative theory – narration, story, characters – can fruitfully be applied to new storytelling practices, including the dynamic field of game studies. However, narrative theory cannot account for all the complexities of game production and gameplay, so that game studies is inevitably a hybrid field in which narrative theory is combined with other domains of theory, including cultural studies, design studies and critical theories including feminist and postcolonial studies.

Not all computer games rely on narrative; for instance, sports simulation games imitate physical activities such as car racing, golf or football; puzzle games require the exercise of logic and hand-eye coordination; and music videogames such as *Sing Star* require players to sing along with music videos, often incorporating competitive elements. Players may create narratives about their own and others' performance in these games, but the games themselves are not built on narrative elements. By contrast, action adventure and role-playing games (RPGs) typically draw upon narrative elements in order to invest games with meaning. Discussing the game *Castlevania: Symphony of the Night*, James Gee notes that it combines 'an abstract rule system about shapes, movements, and combinations with story elements' (2006, p. 59). By story elements, Gee means actors (characters), objects that appear in games, the changing states of actors, and events. But framing these elements are the larger systems of narration within which they function.

In all modes and text-types, narration is a complex, polyphonic process. Mikhail Bakhtin, the Russian philosopher and literary critic, says that in the novel various discourses combine: authorial narration, dialogue which reflects everyday speech, interpolated text-types such as diaries and letters, references to other texts such as films and fiction, and so on. While these various strands are 'relatively autonomous' (1981, p. 262), Bakhtin says that they participate in 'the process whereby the unified meaning of the whole is structured and revealed' (p. 262). Added to this complex array of discourses, readers bring to the act of reading a wide range of capabilities, knowledge, tastes and experience which shape their reception of literary texts. What Bakhtin says about novels can readily be applied to the narration of role-playing computer games, which incorporate a dazzling range of discourses in different modalities: visual, verbal, and auditory. Different game genres incorporate particular arrangements and combinations of features, elements and events, from medievalist games, which call on stock settings such as castles and dungeons, and characters such as knights, dragons, magicians and elves, to science fiction games such as *Star Wars Galaxies*, set within and across a system of ten planets and incorporating figures from the *Star Wars* films.

Players who access a role-playing game such as *World of Warcraft* (*WoW*) are immediately situated in what Alexander Galloway describes as 'the game's total world of narrative action' (2006, p. 2). This world appears as a self-contained universe comprising landscapes, non-playing characters (NPCs), music, on-screen text, dialogue, and sound effects. In *WoW*, the player's first task is to select an avatar, who may belong to one of two factions (horde or alliance). The selection of faction determines which races and classes are available; and the appearance of avatars, as well as the attributes and skills available to them, are determined by the game design. Just as readers cannot change the words in a novel, so *WoW* players are to a large extent circumscribed by game design. However, advanced players can develop modifications (mods) such as weapons, story lines, music and characters as well as resources including maps and calculation software. This capacity for players to introduce new elements into existing games pinpoints the most crucial difference between literary and game narratives. As Galloway explains, 'videogames are not just images or stories or play or games but *actions*' (2006, p. 37).

At the beginning of this chapter I noted that we generally produce narratives retrospectively, as stories are shaped by the way they end. Players of RPGs engage with a variety of temporal schemes. Each time they log into games they build on previous episodes of play in which their avatars have achieved (or not achieved) quests, travelled through landscapes and encountered NPCs or other players. That is, their play is shaped by their retrospective knowledge of previous narratives. When they commence a session of play, however, their experience takes place in real time and is typically characterised by immersion in the game (Carr, 2006, pp. 52–57), which may produce the effect that hours and minutes go by without players realising it. A third temporal scheme may be introduced in the form of back-story elements; for instance, in *WoW*, when players approach NPCs to obtain a new quest, they are often informed about events in the remote past. They might, for instance, be charged with avenging a wrong done to a past hero, or recovering stolen treasures. The unfolding narratives of the gameplay thus shift between the remote and the immediate past, and the present of the player's current game. They also shift between narrative points of view: at times players view their avatars as figures in landscapes and thus through a third-person perspective; at others they inhabit the figures of their avatars, seeing events and space through their eyes in what approximates first-person narration.

As players progress or 'level up' through games, narratives become more complex and players must perform more difficult tasks and quests. At the same time, game design affords enhanced game experiences: players may enjoy the pleasures of flying through space, or driving fast cars, or engaging with group projects. In her study *Play Between Worlds*, T.L. Taylor makes a distinction between 'casual and power gamers' (2006, p. 70). Players in the second of these categories typically invest enhanced levels of commitment and energy in gaming. Taylor notes that her study of power gamers in *EverQuest* shows that these advanced players tend to value the narrative elements of the game very highly: 'they ... are dedicated to the back-story and narrative structure of the world. They game through developing characters, alliances, and plots' (2006, p. 72). It seems, then, that advanced players view narrative as a crucial aspect of the pleasures offered by gaming, and enhance their enjoyment by creating ever more complex and nuanced narratives.

Like all texts incorporating narrative, games embody and construct world views and ideologies, in that they are informed by discourses dominant in the cultures in which they are produced. Just as the ideological content of novels and films resides in the 'how' of narrative rather than the 'what' of storylines, so the ideologies and world views of games are manifested through the 'how' of representation and game narratives. For instance, there is a large body of research which draws on feminist theories to critique gendered representations and narratives in games, including work by Taylor (2006), Carr (2006), Jenkins (1998) and de Castell (2007). Taylor points out that many women players who take up RPGs such as *WoW* and *EverQuest* express dissatisfaction with the narrow, stereotypical versions of women embodied in the design of avatars, coming to the conclusion that they 'simply must 'live with' the avatar images – the bodies – they are given' (147) in games whose production tends to privilege corporate interests. Another line of feminist engagement with game narratives is exemplified by the work of Jennifer Jenson and Suzanne de Castell, who draw on Judith Butler's theories of performativity to challenge 'canonical' views about girl gamers, which insist that girls prefer non-competitive games and value cooperation. Jenson and de Castell argue that these orthodoxies merely replicate essentialised views of a static, stable female subject (Jenson & de Castell, 2007).

As well as feminist studies of games, theories from postcolonial and critical race studies can usefully inform investigations into game narratives which incorporate historical events and settings. In his paper 'Virtual Unaustralia: Videogames and Australia's Colonial History,' Tom Apperley discusses how the colonisation of Australia is represented in two historical strategy games, *Europa Universalis II* and *Victoria: Empire Under the Sun*. Apperley argues that both games treat Aboriginal populations as 'homogenous natives to be assimilated as the player sees fit' (2007, p. 17), thus producing an abstracted, depoliticised perspective of imperial projects which ignores the material effects of colonisation on Indigenous peoples. As Apperley also shows, the forums associated with both games show evidence of a high degree of player awareness of the ideological implications of representations, and a concern with questions of accuracy. Thus, players are not passive recipients of game ideologies; but the games themselves are powerfully informed by the assumption that colonisers have only two options in regard to Indigenous populations: annihilation, or assimilation.

As I have indicated, narrative theory alone cannot account for the entirety of game design and the experience of players, but is best used in conjunction with other approaches. Narrative plays various roles in the study of computer games and gameplay. First, accounts of the development of games and game studies take narrative forms: they select key moments and individuals, ascribe cause and effect, identify tensions or conflicts, and are shaped by the values and perspectives of those who produce them. Second, the designs of many computer games are built on narratives which aim to engage players and propel them through various levels of expertise. Third, players typically represent their experiences of gaming, whether online or offline, through narratives in which they celebrate their achievements and identify pivotal moments in their development as players. There is no such thing as a narrative without ideologies; it follows that games, too, are always implicated in and informed by the values and views of their producers, both explicit and implicit. As persuasive and powerful narrative experiences, computer games invite and reward investigation.

Chapter 14

Videogames and innovation

Vincent Trundle

Overview of chapter

Videogames create a new screen aesthetic and new possibilities for social discourse. Videogames are ideal pedagogical tools and are highly engaging for most students. They involve interactive narratives, create new forms of spatial representation and demand experimentation. Videogames are also pervasive in most societies and when all this is combined, they call for reflection, deeper inspection and interpretation. Since its establishment, Melbourne's Australian Centre for the Moving Image (ACMI) has celebrated, explored and promoted the cultural and creative richness of videogames through exhibition, education, partnerships and more. ACMI's education programs have included practical production skills, evaluation and discussion forums, and the use of games for learning. Hundreds of students have engaged in an ACMI workshop that involves using videogames to make movies, known as *machinima* movies. This article explores both the practicalities of user-created content such as *machinima* and how *machinima* empowers the students to consider the place of videogames in society and culture.

Since its inception, ACMI has embraced and explored videogames and game culture. ACMI recognises the prominent and influential position that videogames hold in most societies along with cinema, television and digital media. Even before opening at Federation Square, *acmipark,* the multiplayer game, was being built to complement the real world of ACMI and Federation Square. The intention of *acmipark* was to explore the possibilities of virtual place-making and the occupation of these radical new technological spaces.

acmipark was the first site-specific extension of a real-life public venue to be delivered online, as an occupiable world. *acmipark* was conceived and developed not so much as a game but as a work of art. It did, however, use game-engine technology, offering opportunities for 'play' and 'exploration' – two key words in ACMI's overall approach to moving-image culture.

In March 2004, ACMI opened a space called the Games Lab. It was neither an exhibition space nor was it a library; it was neither a classroom nor a studio – it was all of the above. It was a 'Lab.' It housed *acmipark* terminals and offered curated interactive videogame exhibitions, workshop and talk space and a place to demonstrate new gaming technologies. All iterations offered many different angles of exploration – from straight play, to exploring genre and meaning, to art and technology, politics and humanity, icons and fear. It was a space for games culture, leading an international trend in the inclusion of computer and videogames as part of a serious aesthetic and cultural dialogue. The first major exhibition in the space, *State of Play*, was a survey of games that focused directly on political issues. It used the videogames to engage audiences with a series of issues aiming to inform, connect, question and reflect, with a focus on how videogames can achieve these ends.

In 2009, ACMI opened *Screen Worlds: The Story of Film, Television & Digital Culture*. The Games Lab was relocated into the heart of the exhibition, placing games in a metaphorical nexus that reflects the presence of videogames in historical, contemporary and emergent practice. The games are chosen to demonstrate the French Sociologist Roger Caillois's (2001/1958) four forms of gameplay – competition, chance, make believe, sensation – and consider the ideas of rule-bound play or chaotic play. Through its contextual positioning and allure, the Games Lab continues to attract exploration and play in this important part of contemporary culture.

The rapid rise of the form as both social and economic force cannot be understated, yet its impact on education is limited. The discussion of videogames in mainstream media is typically stereotyped, with most debate centred on the playing of games as a socially remote and isolating activity with an underlying premise of addiction. Despite this, videogames continue to grow, embedding themselves as a dominant screen form on portable devices and inside the family home, sitting comfortably alongside other 'traditional' media forms.

In considering where and how games sit in relation to education I have drawn out three main aspects in forming a notion of games literacy (Figure 14.1).

> **Culture/industry of videogames**
> Here we study videogames as a part of the umbrella of Digital Media Cultures. By this we mean the 'reading' of games. We explore and interpret areas such as producers' motives, representations, genre/style, character, world, social structures, interface/HUD, camera position, story, history and regulation.
>
> **Craft/art of making games**
> This area focuses on the practicalities of production. It could be seen as the 'writing' of games and is specifically an applied approach. Here we look at game development roles such as game design, research, programming, art, audio, production managing, testing, social management and law.
>
> **Using specific games to learn specific skills**
> This is a highly practical approach to videogames as an educational tool. This involves gameplaying to learn or build new, specifically desired skills. Many of the games in this sphere are simulations of systems or environments such as medical arthroscopy or physics testing. Games such as *America's Army* or *Roller Coaster Tycoon* can also be put in this category in that they aim to simulate several aspects of real-world jobs.

Figure 14.1 Three main aspects of games literacy

At ACMI I have explored these areas in a variety of workshops, talks and forums and have extended adoption of videogames within mainstream education by including games as one of the three core elements of the national moving image competition *Screen It*. ACMI supports this initiative with online resources offered as part of the competition and also through education and public games resources such as the *Sonic The Hedgehog Education Kit* and *Kids and Videogames: Parents, Kids and Videogames What's the Score?*.

Several schools have integrated ACMI videogames workshops (*machinima* in particular) into their regular curriculum, enabling students to further extend core curriculum programs via games.

User-created content

Many videogame designers now include options for user-created content (UCC) in games. Here the player is given the opportunity to contribute to the game beyond the straightforward gameplay dictated by the game's developer. The origins of this development lie in the subversion/innovation of original game designs where enthusiasts got 'under the bonnet' of a game in order to create a different product, a different look for, or interaction with, the game. The simplest example can be seen in the way most games now give players a way to customise their in-game characters, with some of the more complex creative options allowing players to create their own game levels and videos of play to share with others. These games rely on and enhance the more social aspects of gameplay, offering the player a community. For the game publisher this promises a longer period of sales as the community grows.

The ability for students to analyse a game and to understand and synthesise its cultural and technical content has significant educational potential. To design a videogame level requires creativity, consideration of audience, ICT skills, testing and reflection. Good free (or very inexpensive) examples of games that have considerable offers in terms of UCC include the *Trackmania* series, *Crayon Physics Deluxe*, and *Soup Toys*. Each of these examples is suitable for all ages. They have a free version that includes preset game experiences. They all have excellent UCC offers, which considerably enhance the experience. *Trackmania*, for example, offers car customisation, track creation, online sharing, and video production (*machinima* making).

Making *machinima* is an excellent example of UCC and innovation, where the technology of videogames is used to create stories – moving-image stories (Figure 14.2).

What is machinima? [Mah-Sheen-Eh-Mah]

The word is a mash-up of 'machine,' 'cinema' and 'animation.' It is:
- Using real-time 3D worlds, characters and sounds of games to make animations.
- Filmmaking within a real-time, 3D virtual environment which requires no expensive camera equipment or software.

Figure 14.2 What is machinima?

Machinima is a relatively new form of filmmaking where computer game technology is used to 'shoot' films. The real-time virtual environment and characters in the game enable visual components (and sometimes audio) to be appropriated into a new narrative created by the player/writer. As characters, objects and scenery of a videogame are manipulated (the 'gameplay'), they are captured as a digital file for playback either from within the game or external to the game as a digital video file. This video file is then treated like any other form of digital video file and taken into editing software and cut together with other shots to make a film or animation. Essentially, the often detailed and in-depth worlds experienced whilst playing the game can be recorded and then integrated into a new film story.

The term *machinima* is unusual as technically it is both a production technique and a genre. You can make a piece of *machinima* and film with *machinima*. Consider a *machinima* piece as you would a 3D animation such as *The Incredibles*; the creators need to make the characters and scenery and then animate them from scratch. Each of those processes requires considerable time, software skills and expensive software. To make *machinima* you need only a videogame and something to capture the action in the game. It is essentially quick and cheap. However, you often have less control over the look, which means that the story must hold the work together.

> Why make *machinima*?
>
> 'Once I discovered *machinima*, it became so much more exciting for me to create my own characters and stories than to simply play the game within the confines of the designer's original creative vision. Now I am able to mould the game to reflect my own imagination and, in place of a gaming clan, I run a production group made up of people from around the world interested in working with me on *machinima* projects.'

Figure 14.3 Why make machinima? From 'I was a teenage machinima maker,' http://www.machinima.com/article/view&id=454 (21 October 2010)

Machinima is reliant on popular videogames and engages those who are comfortable exploring the worlds presented in games. It offers an extra level of involvement in the embedded culture of the game (and often into the wider game community) where the content created forms part of the increasing cultural capital that surrounds a game. *Machinima* offers a constructive and self-expressive opportunity to satisfy that desire. It is a means for people not only to express themselves, their ideas and their imagination, but to do so in three-dimensional animations and without having to invest large amounts of money or learn highly complex 3D animation programs.

Unlike the typical media stereotype of gameplay – that it is solitary and isolating – *machinima* is rarely a solitary pursuit and mostly requires good teamwork and communication in its construction. It is often made using multiplayer games or requires a combination of skills individuals rarely possess, such as technical proficiency and storytelling ability. As in many other forms of filmmaking, *machinima* offers the opportunity for a team to unite with a common goal, to gain satisfaction in the learning process and enjoy the communication of its united ideas and abilities. Beyond that, there is the tangible product to compare to others, to analyse and reflect on.

Machinima, when considered in educational practice, crosses over the three 'games in learning' areas of literacy outlined in Figure 14.1. Students must consider the specific skills needed for film making; and analyse the game used (as most *machinima* reference the games used and understand the construction of the games), in constructing their own environments (levels) and characters (avatars).

Videogames are primarily designed to be engaging. Their popularity is built upon this engagement and their interactivity. These characteristics are what teachers and schools aspire to include in the learning process.

A large proportion of videogames and surrounding cultural material is consumed and created by young people who receive very little (if any) formal instruction or assistance. If we take for granted the creation of more astute and discerning citizens as a core ideal underpinning education, it stands to reason that we need to make a concerted effort to incorporate the study of videogames and videogames literacy into education.

Chapter 15

Gender and computer games: What can we learn from the research?

Claire Charles

Overview of chapter
Common notions about gender and computer gaming culture might involve images of boys playing violent, fast-paced games, with girls perhaps showing little or no interest in such activities. Concerns might be raised about the relative lack of participation of women and girls within this male-dominated practice, and the implications this might have for their future involvement in careers and industries associated with new media technologies. A key question I take up in this chapter is whether or not it is possible to think of gaming culture in terms of simplistic, binary gender patterns. I review some current research into gender and computer games and I consider what it tells us about who is playing games, what kinds of games they are playing, and why they are playing them. I explore the possible implications of this research for integrating computer games into English and literacy curriculum. I also consider the equally important issue of how playing computer games can operate as an everyday site through which gendered identities, and inequities, are constituted, and I draw on some classroom-based research to explore these everyday gendered practices.

Introduction
Over the past three decades, research and popular commentary exploring the gendered dimensions of computer gaming culture have evolved, in particular, since the publication of Justine Cassell and Henry Jenkins' 1998 collection *From Barbie to Mortal Kombat* (Jenson & de Castell, 2010). Concerns have

included stereotypical images of boys playing violent, fast-paced games, which position females as 'objects,' as well as the relative lack of participation of women and girls within this male-dominated practice; and the implications this might have for their future involvement in careers and industries associated with new media technologies (Jenson & de Castell, 2010; Kennedy, 2002).

A key question I take up in this chapter is whether or not it is possible to think of gaming culture in terms of simplistic, binary gender patterns. The chapter is divided into three sections. First I offer findings about gendered usage from quantitative research studies in the USA and Europe. Second, I explore research with women and girl gamers, and what they say about playing computer games. Finally, I examine how computer gaming operates as an everyday site through which gendered identities, and inequities, are constituted.

Gender and games: some findings about usage

There exists a wide variety of popular computer games, and a number of modes of play. Types of games include console games, Gameboys, PC games, and online games. Online games can be played via PC or in LAN cafes, thus indicating the variety of spaces and places in which computer games can be played, including domestic locations as well as communal social spaces. LAN cafes are venues that provide computer access to the public, with multiple computer stations connected to a Local Area Network (LAN). They are commonly used for multiplayer gaming. In some studies, the popularity of computer games outstrips cinema (see Beavis, 2008).

Despite the concerns and stereotypes identified in the introduction of this chapter, many studies indicate that girls and women do indeed play computer games. A recent American study shows that some girls do play Massively Multiplayer Online Games (MMOGs), and that they play for more hours than males. The participants in this study were, however, predominantly male players, at 80 per cent, despite the authors' claim that national estimates suggest girls actually make up 50 per cent of MMOG players (Williams, Yee, & Caplan, 2008). German researchers Hartmann and Klimmt (2006) state that, despite an apparent gender gap in Germany, the picture in the USA may be different:

> *According to current user data for the US market (ESA, 2005), 43% of all videogame players are female (in contrast to the gender gap in Germany). Online games as a 'new' form of videogame playing have been adopted by many female players as well (44% of all online-players are female, ESA, 2005). The Sims' success as a top selling videogame has been attributed to its attractiveness to female players (Carr, 2005, 2006, p. 911).*

Citing the same American statistics, British researcher Marian Carr explains that '40 per cent of all gameplayers are women. In fact, women over the age of 18 represent a significantly greater portion of the game-playing population (34 per cent) than boys aged 17 or younger (18 per cent)' (Stelfox, 2009). These statistics are undoubtedly interesting for anyone who may have assumed a starker gendered division. There are, however, equally significant issues to consider regarding gender and games, as the statistics about who plays games.

Women and girl gamers: voices from research

What do girls who play computer games say? How did they start playing? What do they enjoy about it? What kinds of games do they like? Do they play differently from boys?

In my research with Catherine Beavis, we spoke with young women who played online computer games in LAN cafes, and we worked with a mixed-gender Year Eight English class that was undertaking a unit of work on computer games. The Year 8 class was playing *The Sims* as part of a unit of English work in a Melbourne secondary school. *The Sims* is a life simulation game, which has been described as a 'digital doll's house' (Vosmeer, Jansz, & van Zoonen, et al., n.d., p. 4). Players create characters, build houses for them, and must make sure their nutritional and social needs are met, such as eating, going to the toilet and getting a job.

Research indicates *The Sims* is popular among women and girls. Dutch researcher Mirjam Vosmeer has suggested that, for the adult women in her research, there was a 'similarity between the pleasures of *Sims* playing and more traditional female pleasures of picking up women's magazines, reading romance novels and watching soap operas' (Vosmeer et al., n.d., p. 2). As one young woman said, 'I would create myself and my friends, and if I was in love with a boy I'd create him too and I'd make sure that he came to my house and we would have a relationship' (Lisa, 17). It was suggestions like these – that *The Sims* appealed particularly to girls – that made us interested in seeing how both boys and girls would respond to this game in the classroom. We designed a short unit using this game, among two others, and had students playing the games, and analysing sections of them, much as students might study a film text.

A few girls in our research suggested that they had better things to do than play computer games. Sue explained that 'We [she and her friends] just go out and stuff.' She also told us that she didn't play PlayStation games, or use the internet. 'I'm not really used to using them.' Some of the boys also said they didn't really play computer games, but were more into PlayStation, playing sport, or going out with friends. As Emily and Catherine practised playing *The Sims* in class, they both told me that they liked the game, and that they sometimes played it at home. Unlike Vosmeer's research, the girls (and boys) in our study seemed to like the social aspect of the game rather than playing alone. As Emily and Catherine played together, they enthusiastically negotiated what kind of house to build, and what furniture they might purchase.

In addition to games such as *The Sims*, some girls enjoyed playing stereotypically 'masculine' and violent games, such as *Counter Strike* (CS), a tactical first-person shooter game. It is popular in LAN cafes, and in this environment players can be sitting with other members of their team, and they can communicate through ear-phones and microphones about strategies as they play. In our research with girls who frequented LAN cafes in Melbourne, we found some who enjoyed playing CS, as well as online role-playing games, such as *World of Warcraft* (*WoW*). These girls were just post-school aged, and were involved in competitive gaming culture.

Two of the girls with whom we spoke, Yvonne and Lorelle, both 19, had started all-girl CS clans. Both had played computer games, such as Nintendo, from a young age. Yvonne explained to us that 'after a while I actually dropped into a LAN cafe one day and I just started playing games and I met my boyfriend there which got me even more interested.' She explained that 'when I started going out with my boyfriend he had a clan himself and I used to go to every single competition and I could feel that excitement when I watched them play … and I wanted to join a clan.'

When we asked these girls what they liked about playing computer games, both emphasised the importance of social interaction. Yvonne also described the pleasure of interacting with people in different parts of the world. 'Now you can actually have a neighbourhood of different people. Like this is your place, you can have someone from America being your neighbour ... what makes the game good is really interaction.'

In addition to socialising, these girls enjoyed the competitive nature of CS and gaming culture. Yvonne told us that 'when I first started playing games ... and particularly CS, like ... a lot of guys always ... they bag girls. They think girls are not as good as guys and I just wanted to prove to them that us girls can do it as well.' For Lorelle too, in addition to social elements of gaming, which she enjoyed, competing against the boys was an important source of motivation. She proudly told us that 'I got the first girl's national team to compete in the multi-sets nationals, and we didn't do very well but we showed our presence, and we were sort of important.'

Overall, these girls described the complex negotiations and positionings involved in being a girl in a male-dominated gaming culture. British researcher Valerie Walkerdine (2007) has argued that girls are positioned differently from boys in relation to playing computer games, especially violent, competitive ones. She states that:

> *Many games are the site for the production of contemporary masculinity because they both demand and appear to ensure performances such as heroism, killing, winning, competition and action, combined with technological skill and rationality ... [I]n relation to girls, this constitutes a problem because contemporary femininity demands practices and performances which bring together heroics, rationality, etc. with the need to maintain a femininity which displays care, co-operation, concern and sensitivity to others. This means that girls have complex sets of positions to negotiate while playing – how do you win while caring for others who may lose, for example? (Walkerdine, 2007, p. 48)*

Walkerdine found that, whilst the girls in her research in an after-school 'computer game club' in Sydney were skilled, felt excited to belong to the club and comfortable in the culture, they didn't play as intensely or competitively as boys – instead enjoying the social interaction afforded by games, and playing up to the 'gaze' of the research camera much more than the boys did. She found that their play would be interspersed with conversations about what TV show they had watched the night before, or other social events.

Digital games: Literacy in action

Gaming as a site for the constitution of gendered identity and inequality

Despite some research, such as Walkerdine's, suggesting that boys and girls may sometimes approach computer games differently, gender certainly does not pre-determine gameplay. Instead, what the research shows, is the significance of computer gaming as a 'technology of gender' (Royse, Lee, Undrahbuhan, Hopson, & Consalvo, et al., 2007), a practice through which gendered identities are negotiated and articulated in the everyday. In other words, gameplay is a key site in which gender identities and gender relations are actively, and messily, constructed.

There is not one way of being a girl gamer, and it is important to attend to the multiplicities in gendered gameplay. Not all girls (or boys) play in the same way for the same reasons. Pam Royse, and her colleagues from the USA, group the female gamers in their study into distinct categories – power gamers, moderate gamers and non-gamers – and explored the different playing styles and habits of each group. In our study with the LAN cafe girls, we drew attention to the fragmentations and multiplicities in the girl gamer identity. We found that there were different ways of being a girl gamer that were not consistent between the girls, or even for individual girl gamers (see Beavis & Charles, 2007). So there is no such thing as a 'girl' way of playing or a 'girl' way of relating to games.

In the classroom, games such as *The Sims* may appeal to both genders. The issue for educators, then, is not so much about agonising over what will appeal to 'girls' or 'boys.' I would argue it is about thoughtfully observing how gender is performed and enacted through the use of games in the classroom, and then making some decisions about where to go from there (see Charles (in press) for a more detailed account of how gendered identities and possible inequalities may be actively constituted through bringing computer games into classrooms). In 1991, Pam Gilbert and Sandra Taylor urged English and literacy educators to consider the gendered effects of bringing popular culture, such as romance novels, into school classrooms (Gilbert & Taylor, 1991). Similarly today, with newer forms of popular culture available to young people, educators need to pay attention to the gendered effects of embracing popular culture in their classrooms, and consider whether they are problematic, or perhaps progressive.

Concluding key points

Research literature indicates that girls and women do play computer games, although they are still under-represented in the games industry and games-based careers. In our research with young women we found that some of them seemed to get into games, especially competitive gaming culture, through their boyfriends or other male friends. Furthermore, other research indicates that the social element of games and gaming culture can be enjoyable for some women and girls, perhaps coming before mastering the game itself.

However, as I have shown in this chapter, there is no one way of being a 'girl' gamer! Nor does gender pre-determine the way someone may respond to computer games. What is perhaps of greater significance, for educators considering introducing computer games into their curriculum, is that computer gaming is a significant cultural practice through which gendered identities, and inequalities, may be enacted in the everyday.

Part 5

Resources

References

Preface

Armstrong, K. (2009). From I.A. Richards to Web 3.0: Preparing our students for tomorrow's world. *World Academy of Science, Engineering and Technology*, 34 (October) 954–961.

Brangiere, E. & Hammes-Adele, S. (2011). Beyond the technology acceptance model: elements to validate the human-technology symbiosis model. In M. Robertson (Ed.), *Ergonomics and Health Aspects of Work with Computers* pp, Berlin: Springer-Verlag. Retrieved 11 July, 2011 from http://books.google.com.au/books?id=x8vTk6tJWuUC&pg=PA15&lpg=PA15&dq=Technosymbiotic&source=bl&ots=pJR6PozJ6Y&sig=7LwzwsbvGEYl4DT9vGhmHzYfm5M&hl=en&ei=nRUeTqWXAuSNmQWG14TrB-w&sa=X&oi=book_result&ct=result&resnum=2&ved=0CB0Q6AEwAQ#v=onepage&q=Technosymbiotic&f=false

Bruce, B. (1998). New Literacies. *The Journal of Adult and Adolescent Literacy*, 42(1) 46-49.

Donnelly, K. (2004). How we lost the plot in reading. *The Australian*, November 13.

Donnelly, K. (2005). Cannon fodder of the culture wars. *The Australian*, February 9.

Durrant, C. (1995). Home Page Browsing. *English In Australia*, No. 111 (March) 2–3.

Durrant, C. (2001). Peripherals to Motherboard: Stories of ICT and English in Australia in the 1980s. C. Durrant and C. Beavis (Eds.), *P(ICT)ures of English: Teachers, learners and technology*, Adelaide: Wakefield Press.

Durrant, C. (2012). Whispering to the Hippopotamus about the 'Literacy Boomerang': Literacy Wars and Rumours of Wars. B. Down & J. Smyth (eds.) *Critical Voices in Teacher Education: Teaching for Social Justice in Conservative Times*. New York: Springer Publishing.

Durrant, C. & Hargreaves, S. (1995). Literacy Online: The Use of Computers in the Secondary Classroom. *English in Australia*, No. 111, March, pp. 37–48.

Durrant, C. & Hargreaves, S. (1996). Computers in the English Classroom. K. Watson, C. Durrant, S. Hargreaves. & W. Sawyer (Eds.) *English Teaching in Perspective: In the context of the 1990s*, (pp. 130–138) Sydney: St Clair Press.

Durrant, C & Green, B. (2000). Literacy and the New Technologies in School Education: Meeting the L(IT)eracy Challenge? *The Australian Journal of Language and Literacy*, 23(2) 89–108.

Durrant, C. & Beavis, C. (Eds.) (2001). *P(ICT)ures of English: Teachers, Learners and Technology*, Adelaide: Wakefield Press.

Ministerial Council for Education, Employment and Youth Affairs (MCEETYA) (1999). *The Hobart Declaration on Schooling* (1989) [electronic resource], Canberra, A.C.T.: Ministerial Council on Education, Employment, Training and Youth Affairs.

Myers, M. (1986). *The present literacy crisis and the public interest*. Retrieved 3 September 2012, from ERIC: http://www.eric.ed.gov/ERICWebPortal/search/detailmini.jsp?_nfpb=true&_&ERICExtSearch_SearchValue_0=ED288183&ERICExtSearch_SearchType_0=no&accno=ED288183

Myers, M. (1987). From the desk of Miles Myers: Institutionalising Inquiry. *The Quarterly of the National Writing Project and the Centre for the Study of Writing*, 9(3) 1–4.

Tuman, M. (1992). *Word perfect: Literacy in the computer age*, London: Falmer Press.

Foreword

Australian Research Council (2011). National Competitive Grants Program. Retrieved 5 September 2011, from http://www.arc.gov.au/ncgp/default.htm.

Kelly, K. (2008). 'Becoming Screen Literate.' *The New York Times*. 21 Nov. 2008. Web 29 Sept. 2010.

Chapter 1: Introduction

Alvermann, D. (Ed.). (2010). *Adolescents' online literacies: Connecting classrooms, digital media and popular culture*. New York: Peter Lang.

Bogost, I. (2007). *Persuasive games: The expressive power of videogames*. MIT Press: Cambridge.

Bourdieu, P., & Wacquant, L.J.D. (1992). *An invitation to reflexive sociology*. Chicago: The University of Chicago Press.

Bradford, C. (2006). *Unsettling narratives: Postcolonial readings of children's literature*. Waterloo, ON Canada: Wilfrid Laurier University Press.

Buckingham, D. (2000). *After the death of childhood: Growing up in the age of electronic media*. Cambridge: Polity Press.

Buckingham, D. (Ed.). (2007). *Youth, identity and digital media*. Cambridge, MA: MIT Press. Retrieved 21 March 2011, from Massachusetts Institute of Technology.

Burn, A. (2009). *Making new media: Creative production and digital literacies*. New York: Peter Lang.

Carrington, V., & Luke, A. (1997). Literacy and Bourdieu's sociological theory: A reframing. *Language and Education, 11*(2), 96–112.

Consalvo, M. (2007). *Cheating: Gaining advantage in videogames*. Cambridge: MIT Press.

Durrant, C., & Green, B. (2000). Literacy and the new technologies in school education: Meeting the l(IT)eracy challenge? *Australian Journal of Language and Literacy, 23*(2), 89–108.

Galloway, A. (2006). *Gaming: Essays in algorithmic culture*. University of Minnesota Press: Minneapolis.

Gee, J.P. (2003). *What video games have to teach us about learning and literacy*. New York: Palgrave McMillan.

Green, B. (1999). The new literacy challenge? *Literacy Learning: Secondary Thoughts, 7*(1), 36–46.

Hutchby, I., & Moran Ellis, J. (2001). *Children, technology and culture: The impacts of technologies in children's lives*. London: Routledge Falmer.

Jenkins, H. (2006). *Fans, bloggers and gamers: Exploring participatory culture*. New York: New York University Press.

Kress, G., & van Leeuwen, T. (1996). *Reading images: The grammar of visual design*. London: Routledge.

Livingstone, S., & Haddon, L. (2009). *EU kids online: Final report* (EC safer internet plus programme deliverable D6.5). London: EU Kids Online. Retrieved 21 March 2011, from Marsh, J. (Ed.). (2005). *Popular culture, new media and digital literacy in early childhood*. New York: Routledge Falmer.

Sefton-Green, J. (Ed.). (1998). *Digital diversions: Youth culture in the age of multimedia*. London: UCL Press.

Sefton-Green, J. (2006). Youth, technology, and media cultures. *Review of Research in Education, 30*, 279–306.

Chapter 2: A model for games and literacy

Aarseth, E. (1997). *Cybertext: Perspectives in ergodic literature*. Baltimore: John Hopkins University Press.

Australian Curriculum, Assessment and Reporting Authority (ACARA) (2010). *The Australian Curriculum: English*. Retrieved 5 September 2011, from http://www.australiancurriculum.edu.au/English/Aims

Apperley, T. (2010). *Gaming rhythms: Play and counterplay from the situated and the global*. Amersterdam: Institute of Network Cultures.

Barton, D., Hamilton, M., & Ivanic, R. (Eds.). (2000). *Situated literacies: Reading and writing in Context*. London: Routledge.

Beavis, C. (2007). New textual worlds: Young people and computer games. In N. Dolby & F. Rizvi (Eds.), *Youth moves: Identities in global perspective* (pp. 53–65). New York, NY: Routledge.

Beavis, C., Nixon, H., & Atkinson, S. (2005). LAN cafes as liminal spaces for new literacies, identities and communities in formation. *Education, Communication and Information, 5*(1), 41–60.

Bogost, I. (2006). *Unit operations: An approach to videogame criticism*. Cambridge: MIT Press.

Bogost, I. (2007). *Persuasive games: The expressive power of videogames*. Cambridge: MIT Press.

Consalvo, M. (2007). *Cheating: Gaining advantage in videogames*. Cambridge: MIT Press.

Galarneau, L., & Zibit, M. (2007). Online games for 21st century skills. In D. Gibson & A. Galloway, A. (Eds.), (2006). *Gaming: Essays in algorithmic culture* (p. 61). Minneapolis: University of Minnesota Press.

Gee. J. (2003). *What video games have to teach us about learning and literacy*. New York: Palgrave MacMillan.

Halliday, M.A.K. (1980). Three aspects of children's language development: Learning language, learning through language, learning about language. In Y.M. Goodman, M.M. Hausser and D.S. Strickland (Eds.). *Oral and Written Language Development: Impact on Schools*. International Reading Association & National Council of Teachers of English: (Proceedings from the 1979 and 1980 IMPACT Conferences). 7-19.

Kress, G. (2003). *Literacy in the new media age*. London: Routledge.

Lankshear, C., & Knobel, M. (2007). *A new literacies sampler*. New York: Peter Lang.

New London Group. (1996). A pedagogy of multiliteracies: Designing social futures. *Harvard Educational Review, 66*, 60–92

Stevens, R., Satwicz, T., & McCarthy, L. (2008). In-game, in-room, in-world: Reconnecting videogames to the rest of kids' lives. In K. Salen (Ed.), *The ecology of games: Reconnecting youth, games and learning* (pp. 41–66). Cambridge: MIT Press.

Walsh, C., & Apperley, T. (2009). Gaming capital: Rethinking literacy. In *Changing climates: Education for sustainable futures*. Proceedings of the AARE 2008 International Education Research Conference, 30 Nov – 4 Dec 2008, Queensland University of Technology.

Chapter 3: Computer games, archetypes and the narrative quest

Dart, J. & Hawkins, P. (2009). Teen gamers at risk of gambling addiction. *The Age*. Retrieved 12 May 2011, from http://www.theage.com.au/national/teen-gamers-at-risk-of-gambling-addiction-20090820-es2q.html

Gee, J. (2003). *What video games have to teach us about learning and literacy*. New York: Palgrave Macmillan.

Hill, J. (2008). *Girl gamers are on the rise, so why isn't anything being made for them?* Retrieved 12 May 2011, from http://www.smh.com.au/news/articles/game-girls/2008/05/07/1209839660016.html

Pahl, K., & Rowsell, J. (2005). *Literacy and education: Understanding the new literacy studies in the classroom*. London: Sage Publications Ltd.

Video gameplayers love the game, not the gore. (2009, January 16). *ScienceDaily*. Retrieved 12 May 2011, from http://www.sciencedaily.com/releases/2009/01/090116073152.htm

Chapter 4: Breaking through the fourth wall: invitation from an avatar

O'Neill, C. (1995). *Drama worlds: A framework for process drama*. Portsmouth: Heinneman.

Chapter 6: Literacy, identity and online fantasy sports games

Acclaim Entertainment. (2002). *Kevin Sheedy AFL coach 2002*

Alverman, D. (2008). Why bother theorising adolescents' online literacies for classroom practice and research? *Journal of Adolescent and Adult Literacy, 52*(1), 8–19.

Bourdieu, P. (1984). *Distinction: A social critique of the judgement of taste*. Cambridge MA: Harvard University Press.

Consalvo, M. (2007). *Cheating: Gaining advantage in videogames*. Cambridge: MIT Press

Genette, G. (1997). *Paratexts: Thresholds of interpretation*. London: Cambridge University Press

HeraldSun TAC. (2008). *SuperCoach*. Retrieved 27 August 2012 from http://supercoach.heraldsun.com.au/

Huizenga, J. (1950). *Homo ludens: A study of the play-element in culture*. Boston: Beacon

Jenkins, H. (2006). *Convergence culture: Where old and new media collide*. New York: New York University Press.

Lemke, J. (2007). *New media and new learning communities: Critical, creative and independent*. Paper presented at the annual meeting of National Council of Teachers of English Assembly for Research (NCTEAR), Nashville, TN. Retrieved 27 August 2012, from http://lchc.ucsd.edu/mca/Mail/xmcamail.2007_01.dir/0354.html

Lilley, C. (2007). *Summer Heights High* [Television series]. Australian Broadcasting Corporation.

Luke, A., Freebody, P., & Land, R. (2000). *Literate futures*. Brisbane: Education Department.

Walsh, C., & Apperley, T. (2008, July) *Researching digital gameplayers: Gameplay and gaming capital*. Paper presented at the IADIS International Conference Gaming 2008: Design for engaging experience and social interaction, Amsterdam, the Netherlands.

Chapter 8: Game plan: Using computer games to engage the disengaged

Freebody, P., & Luke, A. (1990). Literacies programs: Debates & demands in cultural context. *Prospect: Australian Journal of TESOL, 5*(7), 7–16.

Luke, A., & Freebody, P. (1999). A map of possible practices: Further notes on the four resources model. *Practically Primary, 4*(2) 5–8.

Healy, A, & Honan, E. (Eds.). (2004). *Text next: New resources for literacy learning.* Newtown: PETA. Print

Morgan, M., Moni, K., & Jobling, M. (2008). Code-breaker: Developing phonics with a young adult with an intellectual disability. *Journal of Adolescent & Adult Literacy, 50*(1), 52–65.

Walsh, C.S. (2010). Systems-based literacy practices: Digital games research, gameplay and design. *Australian Journal of Language and Literacy, 33*(1), 24–40.

Chapter 9: Reading in the digital age

Bordwell, D. (1988). *Narration in the fiction film.* London: Routledge Press.

Gee, J. (2003). *What video games have to teach us about learning and literacy.* New York: Palgrave Macmillan.

Wollen, T. (1994). Interactivity and the new media. In R. Hoey (Ed.), *Aspects of educational and training technology XXVII* (pp. xx–xx). London: Kogan Page.

Chapter 10: *Game-O-Rama*!

Australian Curriculum Assessment and Reporting Authority. (2010). *Australian curriculum English, version 1.0.* Sydney: ACARA.

Australian Curriculum Assessment and Reporting Authority. (2009). *The shape of the Australian curriculum.* Sydney: ACARA.

Bybbee, R., et al. (2006). *The BSCS 5E instructional model: Origins, effectiveness, and applications: Executive summary.* Colorado Springs: BSSC.

Cope, B., & Kalantzis, M. (Eds.). (2000). *Multiliteracies: Literacy and the design of social futures.* New York, NY: Routledge Taylor & Francis Group.

Chandler, D. (n.d.). *Semiotics for beginners.* Retrieved 23 October 2011, from http://www.aber.ac.uk/media/Documents/S4B/sem01.html

Darling Hammond, L. (2000). How teacher education matters. *Journal of Teacher Education, 51*(3), 166–173.

Disher, G.(1997). *The apostle bird.* Sydney: Hodder.

Game On. (2008). Developed by Christine Everly and Vincent Trundle. Adapted by ACMI Screen Education from the Barbican's original Teachers Pack created to complement the *Game On* exhibition at the Barbican in United Kingdom 2002.

Garlic, I., & Jausovec, N. (1999). Multimedia: Differences in processes observed with EEG. *Educational Research and Development, 47*(3), 5–14.

Good, T., & Brophy, J. (1990). *Educational psychology: A realistic approach* (4th ed.). White Plains, NY: Longman.

Hattie, J. (2009). *Visible learning: A synthesis of over 800 meta-analyses relating to achievement.* London: Routledge Taylor & Francis Group.

Hutchison, D. (2007). *Playing to learn: Video games in the classroom*. Westport: Teacher Ideas Press.

Kress, G. (2000). *Design and transformation*. In B. Cope & K. Mary (Eds.), *Multiliteracies: Literacy learning and the design of social futures* (pp. 153–161). South Yarra: MacMillan.

National Research Council (NRC). (1999). *How people learn: Brain, mind, experience, and school*. J.D. Bransford, A.L. Brown, & R.R. Cockind (Eds.). Washington, DC: National Academy Press.

New London Group. (1996). A pedagogy of multiliteracies: Designing social futures. *Harvard Educational Review, 66*, 60–92.

Saussure, F. de (1974). *Course in general linguistics* (W. Baskin, Trans.). London: Fontana/Collins. (Original work published 1916)

Saussure, F. de (1983). *Course in general linguistics* (R. Harris, Trans.). London: Duckworth. (Original work published 1916)

Siemens, G. (2004). *Connectivism: A learning theory for the digital age*. Retrieved 23 October 2011, from http://www.elearnspace.org/Articles/connectivism.htm

Websites

http://au.gamespot.com/reviews.html?platform=5&type=reviews
http://enhancinged.wgbh.org/research/eeeee.html
http://webpaint.com
http://en.wikipedia.org/wiki/Computer_game
http://en.wikipedia.org/wiki/Interactive_fiction
http://www.aber.ac.uk/media/Documents/S4B/sem01.html
http://www.acmi.net.au/games_lab_game_characters.htm

Chapter 11: Including serious games in the classroom

Molle Industria. (2006). *McDonald's digital game*. Available from www.mcdigitalgame.com/indexeng.html

Playerthree and United Nations International Strategy for Disaster Reduction. (2007). *Stop disasters*. Retrieved 3 September 2012, from http://www.stopdisastersgame.org/en/home.html.

Ruiz, S. (2006). *Darfur is dying*. Retrieved 3 September 2012, from http://www.darfurisdying.com/.

Walsh, C.S. (2010). Systems-based literacy practices: Digital games research, gameplay and design. *Australian Journal of Language and Literacy, 33*(1), 24–40.

Chapter 12: Computer games and the after-school club

Buckingham, D. (2000). *After the Death of Childhood: Growing Up in the Age of Electronic Media*. Cambridge: Polity.

Carrington, V. (2008). 'I'm Dylan and I'm not going to say my last name': Some thoughts on childhood, text and new technologies. *British Educational Research Journal 34*(2), 151–166.

Douglas, J.Y. and Hargadon, A. (2001). The Pleasures of Immersion and Engagement: Schemas, Scripts and the Fifth Business. *Digital Creativity 12*(3), 153–166.

Dyson, A.H. (1997). *Writing Superheros: Contemporary Childhood, Popular Culture, and Classroom Literacy*. New York: Teachers College Press.

Fenton, B. (2006). Daily Telegraph campaign to halt 'Death of Childhood'. *The Daily Telegraph*. London. Retrieved 3 September 2012, from http://www.telegraph.co.uk/news/yourview/1528718/Daily-Telegraph-campaign-to-halt-death-of-childhood.html.

Gee, J.P. (1996). *Social linguistics and literacies: Ideology in Discourses (2nd ed.)*. London: Taylor & Francis.

Livingstone, S. (2003). Children's use of the internet: reflections on the emerging research agenda. *New Media & Society 5*(2), 147–166.

Palmer, S. (2010). Retrieved 1 October 2010, from http://www.suepalmer.co.uk/.

Stald, G. (1998). Living with Computers: Young Danes' Uses of and Thoughts on the Uses of Computers. *Audiovisual Media in Transition*. S. Hjarvard and T. Tufte. Copenhagen: University of Copenhagen, 199-228.

Stern, S. (2002). Sexual Selves on the World Wide Web: Adolescent Girls' Home Pages as Sites for Sexual Self-Expression. *Sexual Teens, Sexual Media*. J. Brown, J. Steele and K. Walsh-Childers. Mahwah, NJ: Lawrence Erlbaum, 265-285.

Turkle, S. (1995). *Life on the Screen: Identity in the Age of the Internet*. New York: Simon and Schuster.

Chapter 13: Narrative and computer games

Apperley, T. (2007). Virtual unaustralia: Videogames and Australia's colonial history. In P. Magee (Ed.), *The unaustralia papers: The electronic refereed conference proceedings of the Cultural Studies Association of Australasia conference*. Retrieved 23 October 2011, from http://tomsresearch.googlepages.com/virtualunaustralia_apperley.pdf

Bakhtin, M. (1981). *The dialogic imagination: Four essays* (M. Holquist, Ed.; C. Emerson & M. Holquist, Trans.). Austin: University of Texas Press.

Carr, D. (2006). Play and pleasure. In D. Carr, D. Buckingham, A. Burn, & G. Schott (Eds.), *Computer games: Text, narrative and play* (pp. 45–58). Cambridge, Massachusetts: Polity Press.

Galloway, A. (2006). *Gaming: Essays on algorithmic culture*. Minneapolis: University of Minnesota Press.

Gee, J. (2006). Why games studies now? Video games: A new art form. *Games and Culture, 1*(1), 58–61.

Heinen, S., & Sommer, R. (Eds.). (2009). *Narratology in the age of cross-disciplinary narrative research*. Berlin: Walter de Gruyter.

Jenson, J., & de Castell, S. (2007). Girls and gaming: Gender research, 'progress' and the death of interpretation. In *Situated play: Proceedings of the DiGRA conference* (pp. 769–771). Retrieved 23 October 2011, from http://www.digra.org/dl/db/07311.36536.pdf

Raessens, J. (2006). Playful identities, or the ludification of culture. *Games and Culture, 1*(1), 52–57.

Simons, J. (2007). Narrative, games, and theory. *Game Studies: The International Journal of Computer Game Research, 7*(1). Retrieved 23 October 2011, from http://gamestudies.org/0701/articles/simons

Taylor, T.L. (2006). *Play between worlds: Exploring online game culture*. Cambridge: MIT Press.

Chapter 14: Videogames and innovation

Caillois, R. (2001/1958). *Man, play and games*. The University of Illinois Press. Web. 22 Oct. 2010 For more info go to: http://www.acmi.net.au/explore_games.htm

To download the *ACMI Machinima Education Kit* see: http://acmieducatorslounge.ning.com/group/videogames

Exemplary Machinima:
    Ballad of the Black Mesa http://www.youtube.com/watch?v=nTbL5elVXrU
    Leet Str33t http://www.youtube.com/watch?v=h38s-kyn2jc
    1K project http://www.youtube.com/watch?v=zG5XJY18y-o

Chapter 15: Games and gender

Beavis, C. (2008). New textual worlds: Young people and computer games. In N. Dolby & F. Rizvi (Eds.), *Youth moves: Identities and education in global perspective* (pp. 53–66) New York: Routledge.

Beavis, C., & Charles, C. (2007). Would the 'real' girl gamer please stand up? Gender, LAN cafés and the reformulation of the girl gamer. *Gender and Education, 19*(6), 691–704.

Cassell, J., & Jenkins, H. (Eds.). (1998). *From Barbie to Mortal Kombat: Gender and computer games*. Cambridge: MIT Press.

Charles, C. (in press). Deleting the male gaze?: Tech-savvy girls and 'new' femininities in secondary school classrooms. In C. Carter & B. Foley (Eds.), *Technology and identity: Constructing the self in a digital world*. Cambridge, UK: Cambridge University Press.

Gilbert, P., & Taylor, S. (1991). *Fashioning the feminine: Girls, popular culture and schooling*. Sydney: Allen & Unwin.

Hartmann, T., & Klimmt, C. (2006). Gender and computer games: Exploring females' dislikes. *Journal of Computer-Mediated Communication, 11*(4), 910–931.

Jenson, J., & de Castell, S. (2010). Gender, simulation, and gaming: Research review and redirections. *Simulation & Gaming, 41*(1), 51–71.

Kennedy, H. (2002). Lara Croft: Feminist icon or cyberbimbo? On the limits of textual analysis. *Game Studies, 2*(2). Retrieved 23 October 2011, from http://www.gamestudies.org/0202/kennedy/

Royse, P., Lee, J., Undrahbuhan, B., Hopson, M., & Consalvo, M. (2007). Women and games: Technologies of the gendered self. *New Media & Society, 9*(4), 555–576.

Stelfox, H. (2009). Girls have a big slice of the computer games action. *Huddersfield Daily Examiner*. Retrieved 24 November 2009, from http://www.highbeam.com/doc/1G1-203623808.html

Vosmeer, M., Jansz, J., & van Zoonen, L. (n.d) 'I'd like to have a house like that': A study of adult female players of The Sims. Retrieved 24 November 2009, from http://www.allacademic.com//meta/p_mla_apa_research_citation/1/7/1/5/0/pages171501/p171501-1.php

Walkerdine, V. (2007). *Children, gender, video games: Towards a relational approach to multimedia*. Basingstoke: Palgrave Macmillan.

Williams, D., Yee, N., & Caplan, S. (2008). Who plays, how much, and why? Debunking the stereotypical gamer profile. *Journal of Computer-Mediated Communication, 13*, 993–1018.

Print and online resources

This book includes many projects that demonstrate the successful use of digital games in the classroom. Some used commercial off-the-shelf games – as discussed in Chapters 3, 5 and 8, for example – while a few, like Chapters 6 and 11, were able to incorporate free games into the project. Choosing the right game, or games, for a project is a difficult one and is shaped by a number of concerns, and among them the appropriateness of the content is obviously an important – and controversial – issue, that Chapters 4 and 5 dealt with in useful and interesting ways. However, at this point it is also important to think about the logistics of incorporating digital games into the curriculum. Issues around the availability of particular digital games and gaming platforms may have a crucial impact on how projects may be conceptualised. How this challenge is met will have a major impact on the way that teachers design and implement classroom projects.

Projects built around *specific* commercial off-the-shelf digital games may be difficult to implement unless the right facilities are available. While many schools in Australia have PC labs, teachers need to coordinate carefully with IT staff regarding the technical requirements of PC gaming software, particularly if the game is a recent release or a re-publication of a classic game (e.g., on the same PC, Activision's Total War series, *Napoleon: Total War* (2010) might not work because it required a newer graphics hardware component than the one currently installed, while *Shogun: Total War* (1999) wouldn't work because it was not compatible with the PC's operating system). Even if a digital game that does work can be found, the expense of purchasing one copy for every student (or each computer in a lab) might otherwise be prohibitive, unless a cheaper republished version can be found.

Teachers considering using commercial off-the-shelf games may consider using games from the following reprint series, all of which are readily available in specialist game stores (EB Games, Game) and in some general stores that sell entertainment software:

- Eiodos – 'Best of' series
- EA – 'Value Games' series
- SEGA/THQ – 'Gamer's Choice' series

- Ubisoft – 'That's Hot' series
- 'Big Bytes' series

Games on these series are often older (3+ years old), and have requirements that will – usually – be more compatible with non-specialist computer facilities. Games that are republished in these series are often best sellers (e.g., *Assassin's Creed*), and have a niche audience that ensures the longevity of interest in the software (*Brian Lara International Cricket*). The best way to get bulk orders will be through internet stores, as most shops stock only a few copies of each game.

Another option for teachers may be to use games that are available for free online, either as downloads, or games which can be played in a browser window (e.g., *Runescape*). Games like these were successfully used in Chapters 6 and 11. This option is useful for teachers facing technical issues and budgetary constraints. However, it is important that the selected games be installed on the computers beforehand, or in the case of games played within the browser, that the correct audiovisual software (usually the latest version of Javascript) is installed on the computers. This will often require careful coordination with technical staff.

Free games can be easily found on the internet, although it may be difficult to find games with the complexity required for many of the projects outlined in the book (particularly projects focusing on narrative like that discussed in Chapter 3). Here are some sites where information on free online games is compiled (the latter focuses on serious games, as used in Chapter 11):

www.freeonlinegames.com
www.miniclip.com
http://www.bogost.com/watercoolergames/ (no longer updated)

Plenty of other sites exist, and it is likely that students will also be able to direct teachers to sites that they use.

Chapter 7 illustrates how free game design software may be successfully introduced into classroom projects. Again, a key issue is technical support on-site at the school, as all the software must be installed on the computers to be used. In addition to *GameMaker*, there is other free game design software available, particularly *GameStar Mechanic*. Both design tools are heavily supported by online communities, and while *GameStar Mechanic* has a stronger education focus, not all of its features are available to holders of free accounts.

GameStar Mechanic: http://gamestarmechanic.com/
GameMaker: http://www.yoyogames.com/

The online communities may also be sources of games that can be used in classroom projects, as *GameMaker* hosts a large community where games are shared and critiqued.

Other classroom projects, like those in Chapters 6, 8 and 9, have successfully used digital game 'paratexts.' While these resources are widely available they may need to be carefully selected and tailored for classroom projects. Many media outlets now have digital game reviews, but sites like *Gamespot Australia* and *Giant Bomb* include multimedia reviews of games.

Gamespot Australia: www.gamespot.com.au
Giant Bomb: www.GiantBomb.com

Such sites include many other useful resources, including podcasts and journalism covering the digital games industry. These sites and many others also collate community-made paratexts, called walkthroughs and FAQs (frequently asked questions) that act as guides for gameplayers. These guides will often include multimedia components.

GameFront: www.gamefront.com
GamerFuzion: www.gamerfuzion.com
IGN: www.faqs.ign.com

Finally, there are quite a few useful print resources that teachers may find useful:

Bogost, I. (2007). *Persuasive games: The expressive power of videogames.* Cambridge: MIT Press.
Brown, H.J. (2008). *Videogames and education.* Armonk: M.E. Sharpe.
Gee, J.P. (2003). *What video games have to teach us about learning and literacy.* New York: Palgrave MacMillan.
Gee, J.P. (2007). *Good video games + good learning: Collected essays on video games, learning and literacy.* New York: Peter Lang.
Gee, J.P., & Hayes, E. (2010). *Women and gaming: The Sims and 21st century learning.* Basingstoke: Palgrave MacMillan.

Ito, M., & Others (2009). *Hanging out, messing around and geeking out.* Cambridge: MIT Press.

Prensky, M. (2006). *'Don't bother me Mom – I'm learning': How computer and video games are preparing your kids for 21st century success – and how you can help them.* St. Paul: Paragon House.

Shaffer, D.W. (2008). *How computer games help children learn.* New York: Palgrave MacMillan.

Whitton, N. (2010). *Learning with digital games: A practical guide to engaging students in higher education.* New York: Routledge.

Appendix

Unit Overview Chapter 11
Length: 5–8 weeks. Total of approx. 12–15 lessons

This Unit provides a detailed example of the ways in which classroom explorations of this kind may be mapped against State or National Curriculum Frameworks. Here, the relevant descriptors for **The Arts, Media and Communications**, Level 6, are presented. This is followed by information about other serious games that might be drawn upon in similar ways.

Victorian Essential Learning Standards for **The Arts (Media)**

Exploring and responding

At Level 6, students observe, research and critically discuss a range of contemporary, traditional, stylistic, historical and cultural examples of arts works in the disciplines and forms in which they are working. They analyse, interpret, compare and evaluate the stylistic, technical, expressive and aesthetic features of arts works created by a range of artists and made in particular times and cultural contexts. They describe and discuss ways that their own and others' arts works communicate and challenge ideas and meaning. They use appropriate arts language and, in the arts works they are exploring and responding to, refer to specific examples. They comment on the impact of arts works, forms and practices on other arts works and society in general to meet Progression point 5.75:

- Comparative analysis of the ways that codes and conventions and production techniques have been used in selected media texts
- Confident and appropriate use of media language when observing, discussing and reflecting on professionally produced media texts
- Use of research to support a comparative analysis of characteristics of media texts from selected forms from a broad range of cultural, social and historical contexts

Unit of work can incorporate the following VELS domains: Victorian Essential Learning Standards for **Communication** (Up to and including level 6).

Listening, viewing and responding

At Level 6, students identify the ways in which complex messages are effectively conveyed and apply this knowledge to their communication. When listening, viewing and responding, they consider alternative views, recognise multiple possible interpretations and respond with insight. They use complex verbal and non-verbal cues, subject-specific language, and a wide range of communication forms. Students use pertinent questions to explore, clarify and elaborate complex meaning.

Presenting

At Level 6, students demonstrate their understanding of the relationship between form, content and mode, and select suitable resources and technologies to effectively communicate. They use subject-specific language and conventions in accordance with the purpose of their presentation to communicate complex information. They provide constructive feedback to others and use feedback and reflection in order to inform their future presentations.

Victorian Essential Learning Standards for **Thinking Processes** (Up to and including Level 6)

Reasoning, processing and inquiry

At Level 6, students discriminate in the way they use a variety of sources. They generate questions that explore perspectives. They process and synthesise complex information and complete activities focusing on problem solving and decision making which involve a wide range and complexity of variables and solutions. They employ appropriate methodologies for creating and verifying knowledge in different disciplines. They make informed decisions based on their analysis of various perspectives and, sometimes contradictory, information.

Creativity

At Level 6, students experiment with innovative possibilities within the parameters of a task. They take calculated risks when defining tasks and generating solutions. They apply selectively a range of creative thinking strategies to broaden their knowledge and engage with contentious, ambiguous, novel and complex ideas.

Reflection, evaluation and metacognition

At Level 6, when reviewing information and refining ideas and beliefs, students explain conscious changes that may occur in their own and others' thinking and analyse alternative perspectives and perceptions. They explain the different methodologies used by different disciplines to create and verify.

Additional serious games

V Gas: *V GAS* is a 3D serious game in which players explore and live in a house that is built to mirror their own. Players begin the game by building a profile including variables such as water use and transportation behaviours, heating and cooling practices, food purchases, and electrical appliance usage. Once the profile has been built, the player can begin the simulation which introduces different scenarios ranging from heat waves to mad cow disease. The player adjusts their lifestyle according to how they would react to these events in real life. All the while, the players' decisions are being measured and recorded, and their overall contribution to N_2O, CO_2, and CH_4 to the atmosphere is measured. (http://en.wikipedia.org/wiki/V_GAS) http://alba.jrc.it/vgas/

Re-Mission: The *Re-Mission* digital game for teens and young adults with cancer was released by the nonprofit HopeLab on April 3, 2006. The game is a Microsoft Windows based third-person shooter based in the serious games genre. The game was conceived by Pam Omidyar and designed based on HopeLab research, direct input from young cancer patients and oncology doctors and nurses, and game developer Realtime Associates, among others. The game was designed to engage young cancer patients through entertaining gameplay while impacting specific psychological and behavioural outcomes associated with successful cancer treatment. (http://en.wikipedia.org/wiki/Re-Mission) http://www.re-mission.net/

Food Force: *Food Force* is an Educational game published by the United Nations World Food Programme (WFP) in 2005. Due to its content, it is considered a serious game (game with educational purpose). Players take on missions to distribute food in a famine-affected country and to help it to recover and become self-sufficient again. At the same time they learn about hunger in the real world and the WFP's work to prevent it. (http://en.wikipedia.org/wiki/Food_Force) http://www.food-force.com/

Index

A

action 10, 17, 22, 39, 51, 63, 71, 77, 79, 99. *See also* games as text, games as action model
Australian Centre for the Moving Image xx, 8, 10, 24, 66, 121
Australian Curriculum 12, 84, 88, 92
avatar 14, 20, 33, 40, 48, 52, 98, 102, 113, 118, 126. *See also* character, characterisation; *See also* games as text, games as action model

B

Bogost 5, 13, 19

C

character 7, 14, 26, 29, 40, 47, 78, 88, 106, 110, 119, 126. *See also* characterisation
characterisation 35, 73, 77, 102. *See also* character
Consalvo 5, 15, 52, 53, 132

D

design 5, 22, 31, 52, 64, 71, 92, 106, 115. *See also* games as text, games as action model
  game design 15, 24, 31, 33, 57, 62, 68, 87, 94, 115, 126, 145
digital literacy xvii, 10, 87, 89, 137

E

engagement xvii, 4, 18, 20, 25, 57, 78, 81, 89, 105, 119, 126
ergodic 13

F

four resources model 66, 71. *See also* Luke, Freebody
Freebody 66, 71

G

Galloway 5, 14, 117
GameMaker 33, 62, 63, 87, 94, 104, 146
Game On 10, 26, 67
Games as text, games as action xviii, 31, 39, 48, 55, 63, 71, 79, 91, 105
gaming capital 5, 17, 20, 52, 56
Gee 5, 21, 25, 114, 117
gender 70, 113, 119, 133. *See also* feminism
girls 68, 112, 119, 127
Grand Theft Auto 41, 44

I

identity 9, 18, 20, 24, 50, 55, 62, 84, 95, 108, 112, 113, 132. *See also* games as text, games as action model
ideology 18, 49
immersion 20, 24, 43, 86, 89, 118
intertextuality 49, 88, 92

K

knowledge about
  games 17, 20, 31, 49, 64, 71, 80, 92, 105
  literacy 87
  texts 91
Kress 6, 21

L

learners 24
learning 59
  -centred approach 66
  language 20
  literacy xx, 3, 87
  practices xviii
  self-directed 61
  through games 17, 19, 20, 71, 80, 105
  virtual 81
literacy 3, 10, 54
Luke 66, 71

M

me as games player 17, 18, 20, 40, 49
multiliteracies 19, 20, 81, 92
multimodal xviii, 7, 17, 20, 56, 71, 81, 83, 95

N

narrative 7, 17, 20, 32, 63, 69, 73, 80, 113

P

paratexts 15, 20, 54, 55, 88, 106

S

serious games 20, 74, 79, 106, 150
situated
  contexts 56
  contexts for gameplay 20
  literacy xx, 10, 16, 55
  -ness 19, 20
situation 15, 20, 39, 48, 55, 105

T

teaching 12, 19, 20, 57, 78, 111
The Simpsons\
  Hit & Run 41

W

wiki 62, 78, 81, 83, 84, 87, 88, 92
world around the game 17, 19, 20, 40, 49, 56, 105

Wakefield Press is an independent publishing and
distribution company based in Adelaide, South Australia.
We love good stories and publish beautiful books.
To see our full range of books, please visit our website at
www.wakefieldpress.com.au
where all titles are available for purchase.